Surviving
Single Motherhood

Surviving
Single Motherhood

A STORY OF HOPE, COURAGE,
PASSION AND DREAMS!

Nicole Franklin

WINEPRESS WP PUBLISHING

Some names have been changed in order to respect anonymity.

WinePress Publishing (PO Box 428, Enumclaw, WA 98022) functions only as book publisher. As such, the ultimate design, content, editorial accuracy, and views expressed or implied in this work are those of the author.

ISBN 1-57921-834-2
Library of Congress Catalog Card Number: 2005909811

Table of Contents

The Power of a Testimony

We all love to hear stories of people who have overcome difficult circumstances and have emerged victorious. I wrote my story to share with women everywhere that I understand what it is to survive single motherhood. My story is proof that there is hope for the woman who finds herself in a demanding, burdensome, exhausting situation that she was never meant to be in. I'm here to tell you that you are not alone. Help is on the way.

I have had the privilege of being under the ministry of Bill Johnson at Bethel Church in Redding, California. One of his core teachings is the power of the testimony. A testimony is a verbal or written account of something miraculous God has done. Anytime someone shares a testimony, that person's words carry the power to open the heavens to duplicate that miracle.

By sharing our testimonies, we fill others with courage to believe in a God who intervenes and makes impossible situations possible.

In Matthew 19:26, Jesus said, "With men this is impossible, but with God all things are possible."

As you travel with me through the memoirs of my life, know that this book did not end up in your hands by accident. God wanted you to read about what He did for me because He wants to do the same thing for you. I encourage you to hold on to the hope that rises up in you as you read.

CHAPTER 1

At First I Was Afraid

The lights were low and my favorite worship CD played softly in the background as I tossed and turned on the hospital bed, trying to find a comfortable position. My contractions were coming fast and hard every five minutes, so I asked the anesthesiologist for my epidural. As I waited for it to take effect, close friends and family gathered around to encourage me and tell me how brave I was. I didn't feel brave; I felt terrified, gripped with the uncertainty of my future and overwhelmed by my situation. Although I had spent almost nine months anticipating this moment, I realized that there was no way to fully prepare for the way my life was going to change.

I was about to give birth to my first child, and although I had loved ones there to support me, I felt very much alone. God was with me that day, but the father of my child was not.

My heart flooded with all sorts of emotions. I was relieved to be nearing the end of a long, uncomfortable pregnancy, but I feared the pain I was about to endure. I was excited to meet my precious baby. (Would he look like his dad or like me?) But I felt guilty bringing him into the world without a father. I was unsure of my ability to be a good mother. Above all, I felt burdened by a heavy weight of responsibility, a heaviness God never intended for me to carry alone. I desperately wanted to share this burden with the man who had helped me create the life of my baby boy.

As my labor progressed, the physical and emotional distress intensified. At 7:30 p.m., I could feel the atmosphere of the room change as my midwife positioned me to begin pushing. Aunt Shari, my coach, grabbed my hand and said in her southern way, "Okay, girl, it's time to push!"

I felt the blood pumping rapidly through my veins as I waited for my next contraction. This was what we had all been waiting for. With one last push, I heard crying and cheering as Nicholas Jordan entered the world at 7:45 p.m., Friday, December 12. When the nurses laid him on my chest, I cried with strong emotion that seemed to completely consume me.

After they cleaned Nicholas and swaddled him in hospital blankets, I held all six pounds, three ounces of him in my arms. Tears rolled down my face as I felt my heart expanding, growing to contain my adoration of this child who had been formed in my womb. I had never experienced anything like this, and the depth of my affection overwhelmed me.

As I stared into his big, beautiful blue eyes, I recalled a day nearly one year earlier when the Lord began tugging at my heart, calling me back to Him. I had changed so much since then. In one year's time, God had transformed me in ways I never thought possible.

CAUGHT IN A VICIOUS CYCLE

One cloudy and gloomy spring day, I was driving to work, doing some serious soul-searching. I was a sophomore in college and my life felt pretty hopeless. Apart from work and school, I spent my time making sure I was never alone. I medicated myself with drugs, alcohol, and men. With every day that passed,

I felt myself drifting further and further down a black hole of dysfunction. The person I dreamed of being was dying, and I felt like I was fighting a losing battle.

In my mind, I knew better. I knew I was caught in a vicious cycle and that I could find a better way. But my pain paralyzed me. At times, it was so overwhelming that all I cared about was forgetting. I knew God was out there somewhere, but it had been years since I'd last prayed. I didn't know where to begin.

I flipped through my music and threw in one of my only Christian CDs—the Newsboys. I knew there was one song that could help me connect with my heavenly Father again. It was "Where You Belong/Turn Your Eyes Upon Jesus."

Certain words from the song reached out and gripped my heart. I really did need to know where I belonged. My chest felt tight and I fought back tears as I tried to turn the eyes of my heart toward Jesus.

As I listened to the lyrics, I could feel God breaking through the hard shell that had encircled my heart. I remembered I had aspirations and goals that were higher than what I had been living. I suddenly had a desire to change. That night, I called my best friend.

Kim and I had been friends since junior high. We both desired to serve the Lord, but were caught up in a lifestyle of sin. We were, as the saying goes, looking for love in all the wrong places. I knew we needed a change so I asked Kim to pray about moving out of state with me.

After considering many different possibilities, we finally settled on Baylor University in Waco, Texas. After hanging up the phone, I dug out my Bible and opened to Matthew. My eyes and heart became fixed on the last verse: "I am with you always, even to the end of the age."[1] The words ministered to me just as the words to the Newsboys song had. In my Bible, I wrote down my thoughts:

April 10

Dear God,

    I am forever searching for a companion, for love and acceptance. I know what I need to do and where I will find it, but time and time again I am deceived into believing that this world will somehow give me what I need. I can't say that I trust You to do what it takes to lead me to You, but today I want You to know that I yield everything I can to You. I pray that You will give me what it takes to someday yield everything I have to You.

I had no idea that what the devil had planned to use to destroy me God was going to use to *restore* me.

I would like to tell you that after this encounter with God my life started turning around for the better. But the truth is that although I had experienced a change of heart, my lifestyle really hadn't changed all that much. *Yet.*

ANOTHER DISTRACTION

A couple of weeks later, I went to a party with one of my friends. While there, I met a football player name Ryan. The whole night he whispered all kinds of "sweet nothings" in my ear. He was big, strong, and confident, and he was paying attention to me! At this point in my life, my standards weren't exactly high. I believed that because we both liked George Strait and because we had both just recovered from big break-ups, that meant we had some sort of deep soul connection.

As the night progressed, conversation (and alcohol) flowed easily. As you might guess, we ended up knowing each other very intimately by the time the night was over.

We spent a lot of time together that month. It was as if I was getting my "attention fix" the way a junkie would from a line of cocaine. I soaked up all the attention Ryan was willing to give and enjoyed every moment of it.

The end of this shallow relationship, however, was inevitable. When it came, I did my best not to feel the sting of rejection. I finished out the semester's classes and exams, but only with the help of my friend Captain Morgan. Together we made it through just fine.

After her finals, Kim came to my apartment to spend the weekend with me. The day before she arrived, I woke up feeling extremely nauseated. I had been out drinking the night before and assumed that a nasty hangover was to blame. As the day progressed I continued to feel worse. A nagging thought in the back of my mind began to surface: *Am I pregnant?*

I looked at the calendar, trying to remember the date of my last period. I began to panic when I realized that it had been more than a month and a half since my last cycle. Thoughts raced through my mind and fear began to envelop me. I quickly decided that the thought of an unplanned pregnancy was too much for me to handle, so I ignored the possibility and went to work as if nothing was wrong.

The next day Kim arrived. I didn't know how to share my predicament with her. She had always warned me about my ways with men, but she didn't understand that I wasn't just making bad choices; I was suffering from an addiction.[2] Over the course of our friendship, we had shared many hurts with each other. I knew I could trust her, that I could always lean on her in a time of need. So I just poured out my dreadful situation to her.

The news of my suspicions affected her deeply and we embraced. We cried together, then went to the store together to buy a pregnancy test.

On the way home, we stopped for lunch. As soon as we ordered our food I excused myself and hurried to the ladies' room, unable to wait any longer to know the truth. I stood in the bathroom stall and watched with complete disbelief as the little plus sign gradually appeared. Desperation consumed me. Hot tears rolled down my flushed face.

As I returned to our table, I felt as if everything was happening in slow motion. I handed my test result to Kim and muttered, "I think we have a problem."

She glanced at the plastic stick, then looked up at me. "What will you do?" she asked with deep concern.

"I don't know," I said as a feeling I can only describe as shock came over me.

When we got into the car to leave the restaurant, I pulled out my cigarettes. Kim, a nursing student, yelled at me. "Nicole! You can't smoke now!"

"Kim," I replied intently, "if ever in my life I needed a cigarette, it's right now!"

RESCUED BY JESUS

Before going to bed that evening, I closed my eyes and whispered, "Help me!" As I expressed that desperate plea for rescue, the Lord showed me something I will never forget. It began like a movie playing out in my mind, almost like a dream, though I was still awake.

It was a chilly, dark, rainy night. I saw the body of a badly beaten woman lying in a deserted alley, tossed aside and left for dead. Although I could not clearly see her face, I knew that I was the woman. I was bloody and bruised from the abuse of sin. Out of the shadows, Jesus walked toward me. He saw me in my nakedness and shame. People I had trusted had abandoned me and I was alone, with no money and no shelter. I was desperate.

With one look, Jesus knew I was pregnant. He picked me up, held me in His strong, welcoming arms, and carried me home. When we got there, He cleaned me up, clothed me, and brushed my hair gently until all the knots were gone. He fed me warm soup and sang words of peace into my soul. I fell asleep that night weary, but fully aware that Jesus had come to rescue me.

In the next scene, I was sleeping. The sun had risen and had filled the room with rays of hope. I woke up amazed at how bright it was. The birds were singing and the air was crisp and clean. It took me a moment to realize where I was. I limped to the bathroom and looked in the mirror. For the first time, I got a good look at my wounds. I hardly recognized myself. My whole face was black and blue and crusted over where blood had oozed out of my cuts. My mouth and jaw were extremely sore. I knew it would be excruciating to do even the simplest of tasks, like brushing my teeth.

I ventured out to the living room and realized that Jesus had been awake and busy that morning while I slept. He had stacked up several books for me to read. There was a new wardrobe, medicine, and bandages—everything I was going to need if I would stay there with Him.

He walked in the room with the warmest smile and eyes full of concern. Without saying a word, I knew that He had opened His home to me, wanting me to stay so He could heal and restore me. He spoke to me that morning. He explained that the healing process was not going to be easy or pain free, but that He would be there to hold my hand every time the bandages needed to be changed. He told me the pregnancy would be difficult, but I wouldn't be alone. He said that as I began to heal and gain energy and strength, I would venture out and become functional again in the world. He told me that one day I would be so well that I would do for others what He was now doing for me! I found it all very hard to believe. But in that moment, hope rose up within me. I had faith to face my future.

The scene faded and I opened my eyes, realizing I had just seen my life from God's perspective. I had many tough decisions ahead of me, but for the first time in many years, I felt that God wasn't angry with me. He had come to rescue me. I clung to that promise of peace and tried to get some sleep.

DECISIONS

The next morning, I began to weigh my options. Everything in me said that I was in no position to raise a child. Believing that I had nothing to offer my baby, I concluded that adoption was the best option. Kim had been accepted to Baylor and was still planning on going there. I had been running away from my problems for so long that my first instinct was to keep running.

My initial thought was to move to Waco with her, just as we had planned, and work with an adoption agency there. I could have my baby in secret; no one but Kim would ever know. A big part of me wanted desperately to avoid telling my friends and family about my pregnancy; their anticipated disappointment was too much for me to bear. I was not proud of my current situation and I feared any further exposure.

I didn't want to tell anyone about my dilemma, but at the same time did not want to face it alone. The thought of keeping such a big secret and isolating myself like that felt very empty and lonely. I just didn't have the courage to let everyone know what a crisis I had gotten myself into.

Most of all, I feared Ryan's response to all this. I knew he would not be a source of support for me, but I had to get his permission to go through with the adoption process. Deep in my heart there was a lingering hope that, once he knew about the baby, he would realize his lasting feelings and dedication to me. I secretly dreamed of him accepting the challenge of parenthood and partnering with me forever. But it was just a dream. In the end, Ryan did not have the character to step up and accept the responsibility of parenthood.

I remember clearly his sarcastic response: "You don't expect me to ask you to marry me, do you?" My hopes were dashed as he rejected both the baby and me.

He tried to convince me to get an abortion. I made it clear to him that abortion was completely out of the question. Struggling to maintain my strength and dignity, I held my head high and told him about my plans to put the baby up for adoption. In order to do this, I explained, I needed him to sign some forms.

After we met for those signatures, I never saw him again.

I WILL SURVIVE

For the next couple of weeks, I spent every waking moment praying and journaling, trying to sort out my circumstances enough to make the right decision. I told God that I had made a real mess of things and it was time for me to hand over my life to more capable hands. I surrendered to God and attempted to put my trust in Him. I reexamined my situation, searching for the courage to face my fears and not run away from them.

During this time of struggle, I often listened to the song "I Will Survive", performed by Gloria Gaynor. I found myself in that song—alone, but not defeated. It did take all the strength I had not to fall apart. And God was definitely mending the pieces of my broken heart. Maybe some people thought I would crumble, or lay down and die. But I didn't. I *survived*.

If a girl ever had a theme song, this was mine! I was a survivor and I declared it daily through the words of that song, written in a different time for a different generation.

My fighting spirit began to rise up. The old me was back! I sat down to reflect on the changes that were taking place in me. As I did, I wrote a note to the Lord in my journal:

August 28

Well, Lord, You proved to be faithful to me. You definitely heard my request! My pregnancy has led me to count on You for what I need. I trust You with all my heart and soul. A lot of things still need work in my life. But the awesome thing that I thank You for is that You saved my life. I will be forever in debt to You.

ADOPTION

I had been raised to believe that adoption was a healthy, life-giving alternative to abortion. I had heard many stories of adoption successes and felt peace about the whole process. However, when I attempted to mentally prepare myself to actually hand over my baby to someone else, I mourned deeply. Yet I still felt that others had much more to offer than I did.

Initially, when I found out I was pregnant, I was young and very unstable emotionally and financially. I assumed adoption was the only decent thing to do for my baby. It was a sacrifice I was willing to make.

As I flipped through the family profiles from the adoption agency, I tried to envision my baby in their arms. The process was agonizing. It hurt so much that I began to let myself imagine what life might be like as a single mother. Upon doing that, a new wave of courage seemed to fill me. I started to wonder if God could make a way for me to raise this child myself.

Those thoughts led me to realize that I could not keep my pregnancy a secret anymore. I took a huge step of faith and shared the news with all my friends and family. I also told them that I had renewed my commitment to God and was depending on Him to get me through it all.

That summer, three families opened their hearts to me, as well as their support and their homes. After much deliberation, I decided to move in with my aunt and uncle who lived in Cleveland, Tennessee. My aunt had been a single mother for eight years before marrying my uncle, so she knew the struggles that were ahead of me. They were involved in an amazing church and wanted me to come and be a part of what was happening there. They assured me that the church would welcome me with wide-open arms. I would be able to find the teaching and training necessary to become a healthy, whole person, capable of becoming a wonderful parent. My plan changed from running and hiding to embracing and transforming.

I made plans to move to Tennessee during the first week of September. Kim was still planning to go to Baylor, so at the end of the summer we parted ways. God had us both in His hands, though, and we each set out on an incredible and unforgettable journey. It was hard to say good-bye, but we knew that at some point we would be together again.

TO THE WOMAN WHO FEELS ALONE

If you find yourself alone and pregnant, I would like to encourage you. Whether you have a history with God or not, let me tell you that He has been watching you. He has seen you in your worst moments and He loves you. He is waiting to rescue you. He will make a way for you to do all that is necessary to make the right decisions.

If you are considering adoption, I must say that there are many valid reasons a young woman should make that sacrifice. My advice to you would be to seek the counsel of people who have experienced adoption first hand. Ask God for the support you need in your life to do what is best for you and your baby. He is faithful to answer the desperate prayers of those who are in need.

On the flip side, I would like to address the pressures young pregnant women face today. Our culture and society will try to convince you that, by becoming a parent, you are settling for less than the best. In fact, children are a blessing from the Lord. You will not have to lay aside all your hopes and dreams if you choose to raise your child. In the end, your life can be more enriched if you decide to embrace parenthood. God used my choice, difficult as it was, to lead me down the road where all my dreams came true. He used this season of my life to shape me and mold me into the person I had always wanted to be. He can do the same for you!

Whether you decide to embrace single motherhood or walk through the process of adoption, God wants to restore you and protect you. The only thing required of you is to hand over your broken life to Someone who is willing and able to fix it. Surrender yourself to Him and He will pick up all the pieces of your broken heart. He alone can put them back together perfectly.

Every girl dreams of a life better than where she finds herself now. It might seem like you are a million miles off the path, but let me encourage you. God loves transforming dreadful, hopeless situations into miraculous, inspiring stories. So don't give up your dreams just yet!

I want to persuade you to let this difficult time draw you closer to Christ. Let Him transform you in the midst of this trial. He is on the other side, no matter which door you choose to walk through. Believe that He is for you and not against you. Have faith that you are not alone.

ENDNOTES

1. Matthew 28:20.
2. The "addiction" I mention here refers to my compulsive sexual behavior. Although my better judgment suggested I should remain abstinent, I was driven by a desire to fill an inner void in my heart. As a result, I ended up inviting many men to my bed.

CHAPTER 2

Letting Go

I decided to move to Tennessee and, more important, to embrace the life of a single mother. I felt like a woman on a mission. If I was going to be a mom in five months, I needed to prepare mentally, emotionally, and spiritually. I guess you could say I was in "pre-parent boot camp." What did I do with my time? I worked as a waitress and attended church, but most of all I spent a lot of time in prayer. I focused my energy on forgiving, forgetting, healing, and looking ahead. God had me on a road to recovery.

INNER HEALING

With the help of a Christian counselor, the Holy Spirit began to bring clarity to my past, exposing hidden wounds and identifying the root issues of sin in my life. As I revisited memories of pain, rejection, and trauma, God helped me to extend forgiveness and receive His truth, love, and healing.[1]

ANGER AND RESENTMENT

Guided by my counselor at church and the Holy Spirit, I traveled through the corridors of my past to visit memories that still had the power to bring tears to my eyes and a squeeze to my chest.

Images of my mom drinking flashed before my eyes. I saw myself in a little five-year-old body, taking on the responsibilities of a grown-up. I was angry with my mom for drinking, for hurting me, and for deciding to leave Dad. Even at that young age, I wanted to help my parents. I felt obligated to fix their relationship, to encourage them, and to counsel them. I had the faith of a child and I knew I could be strong enough for us all. I should have been playing with Barbies, but instead I was trying to sustain the emotional and relational health of my entire family.

I felt angry and saddened. I could feel the weight of the world resting on my frail little shoulders.

In my memory, the Holy Spirit appeared and helped lift the burden off of me. Immediately, the scene changed and I found myself in a beautiful field. I skipped around carelessly, picking flowers and singing Sunday school songs. But when I looked back at my parents, anger rose up within me again. Why didn't they shelter me? Why didn't they protect me?

The Holy Spirit showed me their hidden wounds and how they were internally crippled by their own hurts. When I saw the pain they had experienced, I was amazed that they were able to function at all. My anger melted and I felt compassion rising up within my heart.

The Holy Spirit then showed me my own heart. What had once been an open wound was now closed and healed. A scar remained, so I knew I would never forget the wound. But the pain of the memory had gone.

I asked the Holy Spirit, "Where are we going next?" He took me to a memory where I was nine and my little brother was four. Dad was working the night shift and, since Mom had just left, we were alone together. It was getting close to bedtime. I got my little brother ready for bed.

As I was observing all this, the Holy Spirit told me to come outside with Him so I could look at our house from above.

When I looked down, I saw Jesus. He was as big as our house and He was covering the top of our roof, watching over us. When I saw this I began crying. I could feel His protection over us.

Then we were back inside the house and there was Jesus, holding my brother and me in our dining room. He had brought hundreds of wrapped gifts for us. Jesus said, "I brought these just for you two. They are spiritual gifts and I am going to teach you how to use them." Jesus told me that His desire was to lavish gifts upon me. My brother and I dove into the boxes like it was Christmas morning.

I was able to forgive Mom for leaving us, and Dad for putting the burden of parenthood on me at such a young age. I felt healing taking place. Resentment and anger faded as Jesus assured me of His presence and protection. He was there when no one else was.

DISAPPOINTMENT AND ABANDONMENT

Next, I was fourteen, sitting on my bed at my dad's house. After his divorce from my mom, he married a woman who had four children. I remembered my experiences as a teenager during this time. I saw the hollowness and anger in my eyes. I was so lonely, lost in the busyness of my family. My dad and stepmom were newlyweds trying to juggle six kids.

When I went to school, I was like a dry sponge, soaking up all the attention boys would give me throughout the day. I saw Jesus take the sponge and wring it out. He rinsed out the seduction of the day and poured His healing waters over the sponge.

Again I found myself feeling angry with my parents. Why did my dad marry again? Why didn't he focus on me for a while? Why did he take in all those new kids and offer to them what he had never given me?

As I asked these questions, I saw the Holy Spirit drawing my attention to each of the kids. They were all sitting on their own beds, just as I had been. As I walked from room to room, I saw they had tears in their eyes. They were shaking their fists toward the sky. You see, they had been waiting their whole lives for God to send them a dad. Now, they were looking toward heaven, asking God questions much like I had. Why did this new guy marry Mom and then ignore us? Why isn't he showing us more attention?

I felt my feelings of disappointment and rejection fizzle away as Jesus pulled back a thick curtain, and I saw my dad. He was sitting on his bed, staring at the ground with a look of complete defeat on his face. I could see in his heart a desire to be the best father to all of us. He wanted to be a husband who met all his wife's needs. But he didn't know how. So he retreated to a lonely world of isolation and built walls of stone around his heart. I felt compassion for him instead of rage, forgiveness instead of resentment. I exhaled, releasing all the hurts that I had held inside.

A GOOD GIRL

Finally, the Holy Spirit and I revisited a memory of a time at the mall when I was five years old. I was standing in front of a wishing well. I wanted to make a wish, so I asked my parents for a penny. I closed my eyes and tossed the coin. I can still remember the wish: "Please, God, make me good like the other little girls. I don't want to be bad anymore. I want to be a good little girl. Make me good, God."

When I looked back at the fountain, I saw Jesus. He stood there and caught my coin before it hit the water. Then I saw a series of other memories just like this one. Time after time I kept tossing the coins and kept wishing to be good. Each time, Jesus caught my coin. He looked at me and said, "I wish you could see yourself the way I see you. You are completely good."

I had to forgive my parents for not creating a safe environment, one that was consistent and full of love. This unstable childhood was the reason for my troubling behavior. As a little girl I had always assumed that I was just bad. I always thought there was something wrong with me. But on this precious day, the Lord showed me that I wasn't bad. I was a good little girl!

A SOFTENING HEART

When this journey through my childhood memories was over, I sat up and wiped the tears from my eyes. I knew that God had walked me through some very important steps of forgiveness.

During this time of my life as a young, pregnant, single woman, I felt extremely isolated. I could not turn to my mother (because of her alcoholism) or to my father (because he was consumed with his second marriage and family). Forgiveness was the first step, but I was still faced with learning how to trust again.

For the time being, God was the only person with whom I felt safe. Even when I went to church, I did not socialize or make friends. I walked into the building, sat in my seat, and waited to soak in whatever God had for me. When church was over, I left without any small talk.

After some time went by, I felt the Lord beginning to penetrate my tough exterior. God was softening me, doing a deep work of transformation.

September 20

God, I decided to write my prayers for a while since every time I try to pray I get distracted.

Today was a good day of work at the restaurant. I pray that You will bless my tables. In return I promise to tithe to You what You have asked of me. I've never really realized the importance of it, but Pastor has been teaching me and I am going to do my best. I want You to teach me during this time how to depend on You for the important things. I don't need a man if I have You to take care of me!

There are some nights, though (like last night), when I'm here all alone, and I long for someone to cuddle up with and watch TV with. Someone who could rub my back and my feet when they're sore. I pray at those times You will give me comfort and wrap Your loving arms around me so that I might feel Your acceptance and love. If you do that for me, I can make it until You send me a husband.

I realize that You know the perfect timing and I trust You in that. I am asking You to send someone my way who will be a good daddy for my little baby. Someone who will fulfill every need I have as a woman. I pray he will be a strong spiritual leader yet a sensitive man who will know how to take care of me. I want someone who desires a family and who will be able to take care of us all. Please send him soon!

Thank You for bringing me to such a great church. I pray that You will use my time here to heal me from all the wounds of the past. Once this happens I'll be able to move on and be complete in You. Thank You for all the doors You've opened! I love You.

September 23

Dear God, Sunday was so cool. I finally felt free to worship. You know how, unless there's a song that particularly pertains to me, I just sit there and daydream during worship? If I do feel tears coming, I shut down, though I don't know why. Well, this service was different. First, I let myself cry, really cry. Somehow, after that, I felt Your joy come upon me and I couldn't help but praise Your holy name.

Help me to forgive (completely) all those who have hurt me in the past. I also pray that You will forgive me for all the things I've done in the past to hurt others. I know that in my anger I did many hurtful things. I thank You that it is all covered by Your blood and that You are bringing me out of that rut. I am a different person today because of what You've done for me, Lord.

I pray for my baby tonight, that he will be a great warrior in the kingdom of heaven. I pray that he will know You as his personal Savior. I know that if I raise him under Your guidance, he will.

I pray that You will continue to draw me closer to You. Although I might not like how You do it, do whatever it takes to keep me on the right track. I've made it this far and I do not intend to turn back, ever. I thank You for giving me this opportunity to grow in Your love.

Thank You for my aunt and uncle. They are very special for taking me in like this.

September 24

I wanted to personally thank You tonight for Pastor's message on hearing Your voice. I really needed it and it touched my heart. It also made me realize a lot about how You work. I was feeling lonely and scared for a moment there until I realized that there's no reason for me to feel that way. You will always love me and You are always there for me. Thank you!

After reading this chapter and traveling with me down memory lane, you might have some things you need to release right now. Remember, forgiveness is not about letting the other person off the hook. It is not saying, "I'm okay with what you did to me." It is simply choosing to let go of the things and memories that hold you back.

PRACTICING FORGIVENESS

Imagine you are walking down a road, carrying a suitcase in each hand. Every hurt you have experienced in life adds weight to your luggage. If you have a lot of past hurts and unforgiveness, the load can become quite heavy. It will take you forever to get to your destination if you have to carry all that baggage! Forgiveness makes a way to remove the excess load and will free you up to "travel light." Then you can reach your destination in no time, without any unnecessary delays.

We often hold on to bitterness and unforgiveness because it gives us a sense of power. When we were initially hurt, we felt weak and vulnerable. But withholding forgiveness only gives us a false sense of security. It is actually a hindrance to our life's journey.

Because I knew I needed help walking through my unresolved past, the first thing I did when I arrived in Tennessee was to seek out a counselor and a mentor. I strongly recommend that you do the same. Most churches are able to connect you with a person who can help you in this area. If for some reason you are completely on your own, don't worry. The Holy Spirit can be your guide.

I have learned a few keys that might help you along the way. First, how do you know if you need to forgive someone? My personal test is this: I focus on a memory. If a negative emotion—anger, pain, bitterness, etc.—remains attached to the memory, then I know I still need to forgive. You may have to forgive someone more than once. It is often a process and may take time. But if you have a willingness to release those hurts, God will work with you every step of the way, and He will give you the grace you need to accomplish your tasks.

I had a troubled childhood. My parents had good intentions, I know that now. But when I was suffering from the wounds they had inflicted on me, the saying "The road to hell is paved with good intentions" came to mind often! Because I was so angry, I didn't care that they may have suffered too. It wasn't until I asked God to help me forgive that my heart was able to open up to see the bigger picture.

New revelation came to me as I watched the movie *Divine Secrets of the Ya-Ya Sisterhood*. I was amazed at the principles the Holy Spirit taught me while I watched. Sidda (the main character, played by Sandra Bullock) is a young woman writing and producing a play based on her traumatic childhood. During an interview with *Time* magazine about her film, Sidda's bitterness toward her family is revealed. Sidda blames her dysfunctional mother for years of heartache and pain, with no compassion or desire to forgive. When her mother gets hold of the story, she is devastated that Sidda would judge her without knowing all the facts about her own past. Finally, her mother's friends rally to "fill in the blanks" for Sidda, making it possible for her to understand her mother's actions. Upon learning the truth about her mother's troubled past, Sidda is able to come to a point of healing and forgiveness. As I watched the movie, I cried and laughed with Sidda at the craziness of our childhood experiences.

I remember one line in the movie that stood out to me as being very true of myself. After meeting the Ya Ya Sisters, Sidda's fiancé tells her that she's a lot more normal than she has any right to be. *Ain't that the truth for most of us?*

I share my experience watching *Divine Secrets of the Ya-Ya Sisterhood* because a main key in letting go of the pain is remembering that everyone has a story. Everyone has a past, everyone has a reason they act the way they do. Taking the time to investigate someone's story may give you the information you need to feel compassion for those who have hurt you.

As God began changing my heart, I started asking my parents questions. I came to the conclusion that, at the time, they simply did not have the tools to do things differently. They had done the best they could. As Dr. Phil McGraw often says on his TV show, *Dr. Phil*, "When you know better, you do better."

When my parents came to that place, things did change. Their journey of making things better, combined with my process of forgiveness, eventually led to complete restoration of our relationships.

Forgiveness is powerful. When we forgive, we not only change the course of our own history, but the course of our children's history. Without forgiveness and healing, we are bound to duplicate the same behavior that once was so hurtful to us. Our children will then grow up having to overcome the same trials we battled with. However, when we decide in our hearts to forgive, we become renewed. Past hurts lose their power and the cycle of dysfunction is broken. In its place, a legacy of healing and forgiveness reigns.

There are some people in your life that you will have to forgive even if they are not remorseful for what they did. For me, one of those people was Ryan, my baby's father. As I shared earlier, after signing the papers at the adoption agency, I never saw him again. The Lord had to walk me through a process of forgiveness that was completely one sided.

One thing that may help in a situation like this is to write a letter. Write to the people who have wronged you and express how deeply they hurt you. Ask the Lord to supernaturally give you compassion for them. End each letter with a declaration of forgiveness. Let these people know that even though they have not asked for it, you are giving it.

After you've written these heartfelt letters, throw them away. You don't need to send them. This process is designed for you to work through your anger and resentment so you can arrive at the place of forgiveness. It is usually unwise to try to include the offender in this process.

APPLICATION

Set time apart to spend in prayer. Ask the Holy Spirit to reveal a time when you were hurt and need to forgive someone. You might be surprised at the memories that pop into your mind. While you're there, ask Jesus where He was when all of it was happening. He will show you what He was doing, what lies you believed, and who you need to forgive. As you go through this process, write everything down. If your thoughts seem random, writing them down will help you sort through them later. God will meet you right where you are. He did it for me, more times than I can count. All I had to do was make time for Him and ask.

ENDNOTES

1. The healing I went through was a gradual process. It happened over a series of weeks. For the sake of my story, I condensed some of the most powerful sessions into this chapter.

CHAPTER 3

Forgiving Myself

As difficult as it was to revisit my past and forgive my parents and others for the hurts of my childhood, forgiving myself for my own mistakes turned out to be my greatest challenge. From the time I found out I was pregnant, it was as if a tape recorder started playing in my mind.

> *What did you expect would happen living a lifestyle like this? You've always known that premarital sex is wrong, yet you did it over and over again. You are spoiled. You are ruined. Your purity can never be recovered. You will go through life learning lessons the hard way. Why didn't you have any self-control? Why did you allow yourself to be used like that?*

Although I didn't grow up in an emotionally healthy home, I had attended church all my life and, as a teenager, attended several different youth groups. I vowed many times to God and to myself that I would remain a virgin until marriage. Virginity became a core value of mine that I intended to fulfill no matter what it cost me. So when I had my first serious relationship at the age of fifteen, why did I give in after only a couple of months of charm and empty promises?

WOMAN, THOU ART LOOSED!

Along my road to recovery, I came across a book that helped me tremendously. I was able to forgive myself for my past compromises and put an end to the tape recorder of accusations. The book was *Woman, Thou Art Loosed!* by Bishop T. D. Jakes. I looked on the back cover and saw a picture of the author: a big black man with a space between his two front teeth. He certainly didn't look like the type of man who could help me with my problems. But as I skimmed through some of the pages, I felt motivated and encouraged to read on. Although I had never heard of T. D. Jakes, my heart knew that he had something good to say to my soul.

As I looked at the Table of Contents, my eyes were drawn to the title of the fourth chapter, "The Victim Survives." I hurriedly flipped to that chapter and discovered a story about a woman in the Bible named Tamar.

The name Tamar means palm tree. A palm tree stands tall above all other trees. It keeps its leaves in the fall when other trees lose theirs; it survives the cold winter and remains green; it is a survivor. True to her name, Tamar had the tenacity to endure the stresses and strains life gave her. If you aren't familiar with her story, let me share it with you.

THE RAPE OF TAMAR

David's son Absalom had a beautiful sister named Tamar. Amnon, her half brother, fell desperately in love with her. Amnon became so obsessed with Tamar that he became ill. She was a virgin, and it seemed impossible that he could ever fulfill his love for her.

Amnon had a crafty friend—his cousin Jonadab. He was the son of David's brother Shimea. One day Jonadab said to Amnon, "What's the trouble? Why should the son of a king look so dejected morning after morning?"

Amnon told him, "I am in love with Tamar, Absalom's sister." "Well," Jonadab said, "I'll tell you what to do. Go back to bed and pretend you are sick. When your father comes to see you, ask him to let Tamar come and prepare some food for you. Tell him you'll feel better if she feeds you."

So Amnon pretended to be sick. When the king came to see him, Amnon asked him, "Please let Tamar come to take care of me and cook something for me to eat." David agreed and sent Tamar to Amnon's house to prepare some food for him.

When Tamar arrived at Amnon's house, she went to the room where he was lying down so he could watch her mix some dough. Then she baked some special bread for him. But when she set the serving tray before him, he refused to eat. "Everyone get out of here," Amnon told his servants. So they all left. Then he said to Tamar, "Come to bed with me, my darling sister."

"No, my brother!" she cried. "Don't be foolish! Don't do this to me! You know what a serious crime it is to do such a thing in Israel. Where could I go in my shame? And you would be called one of the greatest fools in Israel. Please, just speak to the king about it, and he will let you marry me."

But Amnon wouldn't listen to her, and since he was stronger than she was, he raped her. Then suddenly Amnon's love turned to hate, and he hated her even more than he had loved her. "Get out of here!" he snarled at her.

"No, no!" Tamar cried. "To reject me now is a greater wrong than what you have already done to me."

But Amnon wouldn't listen to her. He shouted for his servant and demanded, "Throw this woman out, and lock the door behind her!"

So the servant put her out. She was wearing a long, beautiful robe, as was the custom in those days for the king's virgin daughters. But Tamar tore her robe and put ashes on her head. And then, with her face in her hands, she went away crying.[1]

Amnon was a real person, but he also represents what the enemy wanted to accomplish in my own life.[2] Like Amnon, the enemy had a similar evil passion: He wanted to violate me and destroy my life's dreams. He determined to have me, whether it was willingly or by force. Up until this point in my life, he had succeeded. He used other people to steal, kill, and destroy my heart and my virginity.

> Women instinctively are nurturers, reaching out to needy people in order to nurture, love and provide inner strength. But all too often, these desires are taken advantage of by those who would fulfill their own lusts . . . .
>
> There are many wonderful men. But I must warn you about Amnon. He is out there, and he is dangerous . . . .
>
> It is important that you do not allow loneliness to coerce you into Amnon's bed. Men who have sex with women without being committed to them are just as guilty of abuse as a rapist. A woman may have given her body to such a man, but she did so because of certain expectations. When someone uses another person for sex by misleading them, it is the same as physical rape. The abuse is more subtle, but it amounts to the same thing.[3]

I thought back to my first serious boyfriend, Shawn. What I remembered most clearly was how he desired me. It was almost as if, from the moment he saw me, he had to have me. He broke up with his girlfriend to start dating me and pursued me with seductive intensity. Despite his unclean intentions, it did feel good to be desired and wanted.

I tried to fill my emptiness with Shawn's attention, but it only resulted in hurt and betrayal. Our relationship had stemmed from lust, not love. Shawn had no intention of committing to me in marriage, and he took something from me that was never meant to be his. He was an Amnon in my life. Through our relationship, the enemy tried to destroy me. I was a victim, like Tamar, and I didn't even know it.

The emotional and spiritual abuse that came as a result of my relationship with Shawn left me torn and bruised. My dreams were shattered and my confidence was violated. As I read that chapter titled "The Victim Survives," the words spoke to my heart and revealed what had happened to me.

> [Amnon] destroyed her destiny and her future. He slashed her self-esteem. He spoiled her integrity. He broke her femininity like a twig under his feet. He assassinated her character. She went into his room a virgin with a future, but when it was over, she was a bleeding, trembling, crying mass of pain. . . . Tamar's body may have survived, but her femininity was destroyed . . . .
>
> Have you ever had anything happen to you that changed you forever? Something you went through that somehow, like a palm tree, you survived? . . . You shout. You sing. You skip. But when no one is looking, when the crowd is gone and the lights are out, you are still that trembling, crying, bleeding mass of pain.[4]

When surrounded by friends and family, I upheld the façade that I was doing well. But in my times of darkness, the pain seeped through every part of my body. I grieved over my loss of innocence. I had handed Shawn all of me when I was only sixteen. I had given him my virginity, my youth, my time, my trust, and my hope for the future. However, there seemed to emerge an even deeper cry from within me.

After Amnon had raped Tamar, he did not even want her. After he had destroyed her integrity and self-esteem, assassinating any hope for a future, all Tamar could say was, "To reject me now is a greater wrong than what you have already done to me."[5] T. D. Jakes notes:

> When [you] feel unwanted, it destroys [your] sense of esteem and value. . . . It injures something about you that changes how you relate to everyone else for the rest of your life. . . .
>
> What do you do when you don't know what to do? When you're filled with regrets, pains, nightmare experiences, and are seemingly unable to find relief? Tamar stayed on the ground. And she cried.[6]

I realized that I had done what Tamar had done. I stayed on the ground and cried. I lost my sense of purpose and let my life spiral out of control. My world became a vicious cycle of trying to cover up the hurts. However, in doing so, I created more hurts and then desperately scrambled to cover those up as well.

You'd think after rehashing so much unhappiness, I would have felt regretful and desperate. But there was something about discovering I was a victim that set me free. I started seeing a light at the end of my tunnel. I had an incredible feeling that God specifically had me in mind when He inspired T. D. Jakes to write his book. I closed my eyes and worshipped the Lord as tears rolled down my face.

While I worshipped, I recalled a memory that I had hidden away, locked up tight in the vault of my "Most Horrible Memories."

A TOUCH FROM JESUS

After almost four years of an emotionally charged, romantic relationship, Shawn and I struggled to get along. I naively believed that somehow we could (and would) work out all our problems, just as we had always done before. I was in my apartment and decided to call him to hash things out. He answered the phone, sounding very distant. I told him I had been thinking about our relationship and wanted him to come over so we could talk. He said he couldn't come over that evening because he was taking his new girlfriend to a softball game.

A sick feeling came over me as I scrambled to reply with some dignity. I knew he had spent time with this girl, but I felt confident that our bond would overcome any little fling he might have. *He's just trying to make me jealous,* I reasoned to myself.

As he began to close the conversation, I felt myself reeling. This couldn't be the end. Four years was too much time, too much love to just throw away. My heart was pounding so loud I was afraid he'd be able to hear it through the phone. Tears welled up in my eyes. I heard his voice say, "Good-bye." When the phone hit the receiver, I collapsed. There I was—a trembling, devastated mass on the floor, with only coarse carpet underneath to comfort me.

From a distance, I watched myself in the memory. As I revisited my pain and heartbreak, I heaved with sobs full of grief and sorrow. I had visited this memory before, but never lingered long because it was just too awful. This time, however, I felt I was supposed to stay.

As I waited, I saw something I had never seen before. Jesus appeared. He was sitting there, right on the floor next to me. I thought I saw something in His eyes, but I couldn't tell for sure. As I moved in closer to see His face, I was amazed at what was unfolding before me. He had tears in his eyes. My mouth opened in unbelief as I realized that as I was lying there shaking uncontrollably, Jesus sat right next to me with His own sadness overcoming Him. He was crying for me! He put His arms around me and pulled me in close until my head rested on His chest. He wiped away my tears, and then His own.

After a short time, He squeezed me tight and said, "I'm so sorry he broke your heart. I'm so sorry he abandoned you. But

I'm here, and guess what? I love you so much, I will never do that to you. I know you miss him, but I have something so much better for you. You just wait and see."

I opened my eyes and I was so overcome with the amount of love and sympathy I felt from God I couldn't move. I felt His passion for me, something I had never felt before. I never in my wildest dreams imagined that He was hurting *with* me and *for* me that day. I had been in a sinful relationship! I never expected His compassion in the midst of my rejection. I knew now that He had seen me in the most desperate of times, and yet He still wanted me.

For the first time in my life, I was filled with understanding. I didn't have to be perfect for the Lord to accept me, love me, and have compassion for me. All my false concepts of God the Father were now exposed. I had believed that He was disappointed in me, waiting in heaven for me to somehow "get my act together." But now, I saw Him as patiently watching, just waiting for the moment when I was alone. He was yearning to comfort me, yearning to hold me. He said, "I'll wait, no matter how long it takes. I will wait for you, My beloved, to come to Me."

Can you see that He has been waiting for you too? He's not mad at you. He is waiting patiently for you to turn to Him. It doesn't matter where you've been, what you've done, or to whom you've given yourself. He is waiting!

RESTORATION AND RENEWED VISION

Listen carefully to the words God speaks to you:

My daughter, I've been watching you.
I've seen you in your weakest moments—
Desperate for love, desperate to not feel pain and
loneliness.
And now you're here.

He left you, but I never will.
He didn't see your value, the amazing treasure that I created
you to be.
He didn't see it, but I do.
I'm here to pick up the pieces.
I'm here to show you your destiny.

As you meditate on those precious words from God, allow me to speak healing into your soul right now in the name of Jesus. I declare renewed purpose and restoration to come to your life. Now that you know your Daddy in heaven is here to rescue you, I pray you will run furiously into His arms. Let Him hold you; let Him wash away the mistakes of your past. In the Father's embrace, you will recover all that was stolen from you. God the Father will give you back your innocence, your vulnerability, your dignity, and your purity. He can even redeem the time that you lost. "He knows the woman you would have been, the woman you should have been, and the woman you could have been."[7] God will not only restore you to what you were before you encountered your Amnon, He will restore you to the vision He originally placed within you when He created you.

As you read and reread these words, you may feel a change taking place in your spirit.

I remember when I first experienced deliverance and healing in this area. As wonderful as it all was, there was one fear that lingered in the back of my mind. I had many obstacles to overcome, and in the face of it all, I felt spiritually and emotionally handicapped. I often wondered, *How much time is this healing process going to take? years? months? weeks?* I feared the unknown. However, as I remembered everything that God had shown me, a peace and reassurance came over me and I rested in His presence.

I claim that same peace for you right now. Just as I knew I had made it this far and there was no turning back, I know the same is true for you. I was a survivor. You're a survivor. Claim my victory as your own!

October 6

Dear God,

There's so much I need to write down. I hope my hand doesn't fall off!

First things first. This weekend was awesome. I am so glad You met me in the way You did. I felt so many things released from me, and it felt so good to cry. Every time I encounter You in this way I feel another chunk of pain gets taken away. I know You spoke to me, and it encouraged me so much. I know You haven't forgotten me.

I've been thinking a lot about the past few months and how You orchestrated my every move to bring me to this place. That just shows me how much You really care for me. Thanks for taking the time to show me Your love. God, keep reminding me that Your hand is in all of this and You will be faithful. I know You've been hearing my wants and my needs, and I know You would never keep anything away from me that was good. So today I just want to let You know I won't give up. I'm going to see this through to the end without getting discouraged. I know that with You by my side all things are possible.

I messed up, God, but I know You're strong enough and big enough to carry me through it. I am holding You close to my heart and not letting go!

November 29

Dear God,

Last Wednesday night Pastor asked me to be one of the people who shared about what I am thankful for this Thanksgiving. You know how much You've done for me, and it was a privilege to be able to get up there and tell my story, how You saved my life. Afterward Pastor prophesied over me and the baby and said that we would someday touch many people's lives and our story would bring healing to their hearts.

Thank You for being faithful to me even when I'm not faithful. You're teaching me new things every week and I love it. I pray for my precious baby tonight. Give him sweet dreams and help me to have quality rest. I love You!

FORGIVING YOU

Imagine you are in a room where on the wall are the faces of all the people who have hurt you in the past. Now imagine each one of them disappearing. Poof! Poof! Poof!

Just as you see one of the last faces dissolving from the wall, you realize that one large face remains: your own. The Bible tells us that once we ask forgiveness from our Father in heaven for our sin, it is tossed in the sea of forgetfulness. God has no memory of sins for which you have asked forgiveness. The challenge is this: to adopt this same attitude for yourself.

Learn from your mistakes, strive to be pure, and don't hold on to things that God has already forgotten. It may feel foreign to you at first. Even if you just did yesterday that thing you swore you would never do again, today is a new day. All things old have passed away and you have been given a clean slate.[8] People don't always forget easily, but with God, it's a snap.

Once you are able to forgive yourself, your image disappears from the wall and Jesus appears. He tells you He was there all along, you just couldn't see Him. Keep this room clean and you will always see Him.

ENDNOTES

1. See 2 Samuel 13:1–19
2. Whenever I use the word *enemy*, I am referring to the enemy of my soul—Satan.
3. T. D. Jakes, *Woman, Thou Art Loosed! Healing the Wounds of the Past* (Tulsa, OK: Albury Publishing, 1996), pp. 64–65.
4. Ibid., p. 73.
5. 2 Samuel 13:16 (NLT).
6. T. D. Jakes, pp. 73–74.
7. Ibid., p. 76.
8. See 2 Corinthians 5:17.

CHAPTER 4

You Live, You Learn

After I gave birth to Nicholas, the nurses wheeled me into the recovery room, where I slept soundly. My dad stayed in the room with me the entire time. It meant so much to have him there with me. When I couldn't hold the baby, he did, and I could see the pride in his eyes as he gazed at Nicholas and prayed over him. Nicholas was his first grandson, and I sensed that there was a special bond between them.

After my hospital stay, my father remained a few more days to help me settle in at home. I would not be alone when he left. My aunt and uncle would be there to help. But I was having great difficulty preparing myself to say good-bye to him. As we began to express how much we would miss each other, I completely broke down. He held me and asked me why I was having such a hard time. I couldn't explain why, I just begged him to stay a little longer. He was so moved by my emotion that he made arrangements to stay one more day. I still cried when he left, but that little bit of extra time definitely made a difference.

After his departure a loneliness swept over me that I hadn't been prepared for. Even though I had walked through forgiveness, I felt extremely sad that my dad was too busy to take care of me and my new baby. I still had to deal with feelings of abandonment. I asked the Lord to show me that He was there to take care of us. It wasn't easy, but eventually I could feel His presence with us.

It took a few weeks for the reality of single motherhood to sink in. My first Christmas with Nicholas came and went. After the excitement of the holidays wore off, I hit a bit of a slump. There were nights when I longed for a break. Nicholas was a good baby, but it was quite an adjustment to get up three, four, and five times a night to attend to him. Sometimes during those lonely night feedings, bitter tears soaked my pillow. My days were spent fantasizing that my "knight in shining armor" would soon come to whisk me away.

I felt very vulnerable during this time in my life. When I was pregnant, I spent all my time and energy picking up the pieces of my life and reestablishing my relationship with God. I had walked through healing and forgiveness and searched out my identity in Christ. But now it seemed as if my focus was shifting.

In the past, I always drifted toward the wrong kind of men. So I determined to find a godly man in church, a man who passionately pursued God and His purposes for his life.

I honestly desired to make God my source, realizing that a husband would be an added bonus. But despite my best intentions, I was driven by emotions that distracted me from the Lord. I had been taught that God was the only One who could fulfill me and make me whole, but somehow that teaching had not completely pierced my heart and become my reality. I felt torn and conflicted. My desire was for God and I spent much time in prayer, but my life played out differently as my actions reflected hidden motives. I guess I was trying to keep secrets from God but not intentionally. In my mind I rationalized certain ideas, and I did not ask God if they were accurate.

For example, I spent a lot of time racked with guilt over the fact that my child had started life without a father. I believed in grace and forgiveness, but I also believed that there were consequences for my sin. In my opinion, from the day of his birth, Nicholas had the cards stacked against him. I would envision him at different stages of his life, and what I saw was never good. It was as if there existed a big, blinking red arrow pointing back to the day when I joined myself with a man outside of marriage. I felt I had compromised my child's future by joining myself with a man who didn't have what was required to step up and be a father. I believed that Nicholas would always struggle with rejection and rebellion, and I constantly wondered how I could help him avoid living a destructive, disastrous life.

I decided that, since I had gotten us into this mess, I would be the one to get us out. I developed a plan that would solve all our problems: I would find a man worthy of being a father for Nicholas and a husband for me. I would make sure to marry him before Nicholas was old enough to realize that he had begun his life without a daddy. By my calculations, I had about three years to make it all happen.

When I considered my options in the dating scene, some cold realizations hit me. Over the course of my life, I had heard men talk about single women who had children. I had seen movies and knew society's overall opinion. According to them, women with children had "extra baggage." I came to the conclusion that most men would steer clear of me when they learned of my situation unless God intervened. I sincerely believed that the man God had for us would fall in love with Nicholas and want to pursue a relationship with me. That would be my sign, my way of knowing it was a "God thing."

In reality, I was just a vulnerable young woman who was still emotionally, spiritually, and physically fragile after just giving birth. I had never been exposed to lasting, unconditional love, and I was secretly burdened with guilt and anxiety about the emotional health of my child. Not only had I given God a very limited timetable to work it all out (without really consulting Him on the matter), but I had drawn up a foolproof way of knowing exactly whom I would marry. Or so I thought.

SET UP FOR FAILURE

Little did I know, I had set myself up for failure. My mind was a war zone. Two opposing forces battled within me. On one hand, I was a calm, rational woman who was pursuing God with all her heart and patiently waiting for the right man to come along and add to her and her son's lives. One the other hand, I was a frenzied, panicked mom, looking for that special someone who would fill in the gaps and make up for lost time.

The enemy was lurking behind every thought. He was scheming and plotting, devising a plan to give me everything I thought I wanted. But his plan was just a counterfeit, a crude knockoff of what my heavenly Father had waiting for me. My enemy knew my doubts and fears—he himself had planted them within me. He stirred up anxiety whenever he could, hissing lies of destruction into my ear with every day that passed. He spent his days and nights orchestrating elaborate traps for me, longing for me to take the bait and fall flat on my face. How I wish I could have seen what was waiting for me just around the corner!

January 16
(my first entry after Nicholas's birth)

Dear Jesus,

I just wanted to tell You tonight that I am feeling quite alone. I need to be able to depend on You, not just for my physical needs here on earth, but also for the deep desires in my heart for relationship. You know how confused I get sometimes, wondering if I should desire to be married or if I should just focus on being content with You, God. All my life I've tried to put my trust and faith into other people and I've continually been let down. I wanted so desperately for certain people to love me, and I was always so devastated when they didn't. Please help me to look to You every time to receive that perfect, unconditional love. Help me to learn how to receive it and feel it.

I need Your loving arms around me. I need to feel the warmth of Your touch. You made us to desire that touch. God, I need You to touch me to the point where I don't have to wonder if it was just my imagination. If You can move mountains and do miracles, then surely You can do this for me.

Sometimes I get so lonely. I want to meet my husband soon. But more than that, I want to seek You until I really find You. I'm not prepared to settle for a lukewarm relationship anymore. I am a passionate person and You made me that way, God. Now I need You to fill up my whole life with You. A husband would be nice, but You would be better. I'm really serious about this. You have been faithful to me in the past, answering my prayers. So just let me know what I need to do. Speak to me, God.

I guess I'd better go to bed; it's getting late. Bless my dreams tonight, Lord. Send all Your angels to protect my thoughts and me. Only allow dreams to bring me closer to You. Don't let them be used to drag up old memories to haunt me.

I pray for Nicholas. Send all Your angels to protect him, too, sparing none. Protect my precious little boy and bless his dreams.

I love You with all my heart, Lord. I marvel at all You've done in my life.

NEW RELATIONSHIPS

After Nicholas's birth, I began to get to know more people in the church. I felt more social and desired to form new and lasting friendships. One of the first people I befriended was a woman named Jaime. Although she was a bit older than I, we hit it off right away. Jaime was quite the extrovert, and I enjoyed being around her because she always brought a smile to my face.

Right after New Year's, Jaime's brother-in-law Michael made his way to Tennessee. Michael had gotten into some trouble with the law, and his probation orders stated that he was to be released into Jaime and her husband's custody. Michael was my age, and after only a few weeks of seeing him at church, I heard rumors that he was interested in me.

One Sunday, Jaime introduced us and my interest was piqued. Although he wasn't the type of guy I had dated in the past, I saw something humble and genuine within him. I could tell he had learned a lot from his recent failures and that he was on the road to recovery, pursuing God and trying to get a fresh start in life.

I hadn't given him much thought, though, until one night, when my opinion of him dramatically changed.

My aunt and uncle were out of town for the weekend and I came down with the flu. Feeling sick and weak, I was struggling to take care of Nicholas, so I called Jaime to see if there was any way she could help me out with the baby. She invited me over to the house so I could rest while she took care of Nicholas. She even insisted that I spend the night in the guest room. I was relieved to have someone to help me, and I gratefully accepted her invitation.

That evening, we all sat and visited, getting to know one another better. Michael sat on the couch across from me. Nicholas was passed around to everyone in the room, including Michael. He seemed to be really good with him and wasn't nervous about the fact that Nicholas, still a newborn, was so tiny. Michael and I swapped stories of our past, and as my medicine kicked in, I became very drowsy.

The next thing I knew, it was six a.m. I was a little disoriented when I realized I had fallen asleep on the couch. It suddenly occurred to me that I had not gotten up with Nicholas at all during the night. I looked across the room with groggy eyes and saw something that made my heart melt. Michael lay there on the other couch, sleeping. Nicholas was curled up on his chest, sound asleep. On the floor near them I saw an empty bottle and Nicholas's diaper bag. I realized that Michael had held the baby all through the night, getting up with him to feed and change him. And he had done it all without waking me.

I was absolutely stunned. This was the most romantic thing any man had ever done for me in my entire life.

But I had just met Michael. Though I knew little bits of his history, I didn't know anything about his goals, dreams, or walk with the Lord. But after what he had done for me that night, I honestly didn't care! If I could have served him my heart on a platter right then and there, I would have. His actions had pierced me to the core.

It is said that the way to a man's heart is through his stomach. Well, the way to a single mom's heart is through her children! Even though I had not previously felt drawn to Michael in a romantic way, he had won me over. This was the sign I'd been waiting for. God had just given me full permission to fall head over heals. At least, that's what I believed.

January 20

Jesus, I have so much to record. First, I want to thank You for meeting me tonight in my time of devotions with You. Reading Your powerful Word makes me want to draw nearer to You. I love You so much and my desire is to know You better than I know myself. Men have let me down my whole life, but You have always been faithful. Please, Lord, draw me closer to You. I give You the authority to do whatever it takes to bring me closer.

You have done so much for me, and I realize that I'll never be able to repay, so I'll just receive it all. I will always thank You from the bottom of my heart. Thank You for providing for me and my son, and thank You for giving me such a perfect little boy. I finally feel like my life is on track again. I'm happy, Lord, and I owe it all to You. You have given me joy, and that has been the most awesome gift to me.

If Michael is "the one" for me, let me know. Prepare both of our hearts so that one day we can be joined for Your glory. It means so much to know that he cares about me. For some reason, I feel a warmth inside about him. That's the only way I can explain it. When I think of him I feel warm and peaceful. But if he's not for me, that's okay. I will trust You.

But, please, Lord, if this is not Your will, send that special person soon. I desire a partner to share my life with, to share my dreams with, and to be a father for my precious little boy. He deserves it. He was so innocent and didn't deserve to be rejected by his father. I don't understand that. How could anyone reject this little boy? He's so lovable. I just don't get it.

If I have mountains to overcome still, show me what they are, Cord, so I may speak to them and tell them to get out of my way!

January 29

Dear God,

Tonight was awesome, wasn't it? I want to write down what happened so I don't forget. The last time I wrote was when You had me reading out of Genesis. For a little while I couldn't think of a reason why that whole chapter applied to me. But tonight I figured it out.

Pastor's message was centered around the story about Rebecca. Afterward we had a time of communion and a private wedding ceremony to symbolize the importance of our commitment to You, Cord. I remembered again Your awesome promise to be faithful to me. When I thought others would be and they weren't, You would be always. So I decided to vow to You, just like I would in a marriage ceremony, to be faithful to You, to honor and worship You.

Concerning Michael, I feel that You have called me to seek out my answer in prayer. God, I really want to know what You think about him and about us. I will trust You to tell me what I need to know about him.

I love You so much, Cord.

During this time, two motivations were driving me, and I was trying to find a balance between them. I pursued God and everything He had for me, but I also pursued a relationship with Michael. Since I was walking with God, trying to do things "the right way," I believed God was supporting me 100 percent.

My aunt and uncle tried to give me advice during this time, suggesting that Michael and I remain friends and take things slow because we were both in a season of recovery. I felt as if they were trying to control me. Things often became tense between us, and I rebelled against their counsel.

Near the end of February, Michael and I began to talk openly about the possibility of marriage. As I shared my thoughts and plans with our pastor, he patiently listened to me and tried to guide me. Just like my aunt and uncle, he suggested that Michael and I take things very slowly.

Toward the middle of March, I began to feel a shift take place in my relationship with Michael. It seemed as if we had hit a wall. As things began to get more difficult, I was convinced that the enemy was out to steal my joy. By this time, I was almost positive that God's will was for me to marry Michael. He loved Nicholas and continually proclaimed his love and commitment to me as well. But my heart was growing concerned.

March 18

Dear God,

Tonight is very hard for me. There's something going on with Michael and it doesn't rest well with my spirit. I think he's hiding something from me. What should I do about this, Lord? How do I handle it? Do I come boldly to him and say, "Hey, if you can't be honest with me, then you're out the door"? Or do I approach him quietly and say, "I just can't shake this feeling that there's something wrong between us"?

Lord, I believe You've given me this check in my spirit, just like You did in past relationships. I promised myself I would never ignore it again if I ever felt like a man was hiding something from me. I promise, if he lies to me tonight, I am gone forever. So if he's the one You have chosen for me, then let him know that this is the deciding factor on whether the relationship continues or not.

Help me with this decision, Lord. Do I give him the benefit of the doubt? Or do I dump him without hesitation if he doesn't cough up the truth?

March 22

Dear Jesus,

Well, I talked to Michael about my fears, and he had an explanation for everything. But Lord, I have felt uneasiness and restlessness in my heart for a couple of months now. I can't figure out what it is all about. It just feels like something isn't right.

There are a lot of things going on with my family right now. My fourteen-year-old brother is doing drugs, my mom is still drinking. Perhaps that is the source of my uneasiness.

As I end this time in prayer I want to ask You for a few things. Please prepare me for marriage. Make me a Proverbs 31 woman. Help me to love Michael the way you desire me to. And help us stay strong in keeping our physical relationship pure, appropriate, and limited.

I would also like You to prepare Michael for marriage. Lord, make his desire for You burn strong so that he may never stop seeking You. When we do get married, I know we are not going to have a lot of money, but that doesn't really matter to me. I just pray that our home will be filled with Your glory because that is what is really important.

Next, I would like to pray for my future in ministry. I would like Your spirit and Your love to pour out from me onto others. I feel like my ministry will be my testimony. I feel a strong desire to reach out to young girls who feel they are alone.

I also ask for your protection over my brother and mom. Be with them as I know they are hurting now, Lord.

March 30

Dear Jesus,

Please guide my steps in this dating relationship with Michael. If I mess up, show me. Convict me and let me know if I've done anything wrong. Right now there is a fear inside me about this relationship. I feel like I need to pray a protection over it. Michael is going through a time in his life where he seems unsettled. It feels like he is starting to pull away from You, Lord, and that scares me. Please watch over him and don't let him get too far away. He may not yet be the mighty man of God he is destined to be, but I know he will be. You have done too much in his life for any ground to be lost now.

You promised me, Lord, that You would be faithful to my son and me, and I believe with all my heart You have put the three of us together to be a family.

I became more apprehensive and conflicted about my relationship with Michael. The truth of the matter was, we were both very unsettled when we first met. We had both been restored to right relationship with the Lord and felt like we were on top of the world. But over time, I perceived a change in Michael, and now it was becoming more apparent. His eyes had lost their softness, and harshness entered his voice. After the initial thrill of God's intervention in his life began to wear off, he took back the reins and decided to take charge of his life again.

As I saw these things happening in Michael, I decided to fight for him instead of focusing on what Jesus wanted me to do, which was to release him. God had promised me great things, and it was beginning to look like Michael wasn't going to fit the bill. I just didn't see it that way, so I dug in my heels.

May 12

Dear God,

Hey, it's me, do You remember? I know it has been a long time since I sat down and really prayed. I guess this looks like I only come to You when I need something. I'm sorry about that, I truly am. I guess all I can do is ask You to make me a better person, Lord.

Holy Spirit, I need Your help. I need You to start revealing things to me. Maybe if I knew more, I could do more. I ask for wisdom.

God, I don't have any money. I'm sorry I haven't tithed faithfully. Because of this money shortage, please help Michael to accept me in my regular clothes, help him to love me just as I am in my jeans and T-shirts. I didn't realize until now the pressure he was putting on me to dress differently for him. God, I can't afford to do that right now! Please remind me and help me to do that. Give me the strength to do what You've called me to do in the area of money, to completely trust You.

Our week in Florida meeting his parents went well. I feel like Nicholas and I will fit into his family. It seems like everything is coming together fine. We have been arguing about money lately, especially when we talk about what kind of wedding we would like to have. I feel all this pressure, so I just ask that You will give me Your peace. Thanks, God!

July 18

Dear Jesus,

There are a number of things on my mind tonight. I wanted to take the time to write to You about them. You know the first thing on my mind, and that's Michael and me. I don't know where that argument came from last night, but it really hurt me that he never called today to try to patch things up. We had definite plans today to look for a ring. I have a feeling he went to the lake with his friends and totally pushed me to the side. If he's capable of that, do I really want to marry this man?

Another thing that has been bothering me is the fact that a lot of his bills have been paid late. He makes a lot more money than I do, but it looks like he is really struggling to be responsible with his money.

And in the past four months I don't think I've heard one godly sentence come out of his mouth. In the beginning of our relationship, we talked about our spiritual dreams and goals all the time, but not anymore.

I'm at a crossroads here. I have so many doubts. Is it me, God? Am I being judgmental? I'm not sure I can respect him the way I used to. I used to see great things in our future, but lately it's getting harder and harder to envision those things. Why is it that one week I'm ready to run off and elope, and the next week things feel so shaky? I really need some answers. If he's not willing to be the man of God Nicholas and I need him to be, then I have no other choice but to forget about him. I have come too far and been through way too much to let it all fall apart now.

Please give me some direction in my life about all this. I need peace.

July 22

Well, here's my next question for You, God. Is this the way You're going to force me to deal with certain issues? If I was confused before, You can multiply that by a hundred now. I don't know what is going on. Is this my fault?

Michael informed me that lately he has been thinking a lot about us and he has decided that he's not so sure he wants to continue on with someone in my position. This hurts so much. He was the one who was so eager in the beginning to be a part of Nicholas's and my life.

I'm confused, I'm scared, and I don't know what the near future holds. I have given my heart to someone again, and it seems that he is throwing it away just like the others did. I want to trust You with every breath of my life, but right now I'm feeling like it's time to panic.

I'm a fighter, so I'll never give up. I promise. I've come too far!

July 25

Dear God,

Today my fighting spirit has left me. I am an emotional wreck. I don't know at this point if I'm going to make it.

Michael called me today to tell me he didn't feel we were "compatible" and he wanted to end things forever. I'm at the point now, God, where I don't even feel like living anymore. I wish You would just take Nicholas and me to be with You in heaven. I didn't know I could feel this much pain. I didn't know it was humanly possible. I just can't go on anymore. I don't have the strength; I don't have the desire.

I want to do something so that I can't feel any more hurt. If I knew how to handle it, that would be different. Or if I believed that things were going to be all right, then I could do it. But I am completely broken and all my hope for a future full of happiness has been shattered. I don't have it in me to be a mother, a friend, a daughter, anything. I have nothing left to offer. I'm empty and I don't know what to do, God.

I wish I could pray all the right things right now, but I can't. I feel like I could end things right now. I am that desperate to get away from this pain. I wish I could trust You. I wish I could believe You that one day this will all be okay. But right now, I can't.

As I was writing these heart-wrenching words, the phone rang. It was Barb, one of the ladies in the church who had reached out to me and loved on me and Nicholas. Barb didn't know it, but just then she was a lifeline to me. God told her to call me at that very moment, and she did. I needed her encouragement desperately and there she was to give it to me.

I just talked to Barb and we prayed. "God, I'm hurting so bad right now. I don't have the strength to do spiritual warfare. Please keep my enemies from overcoming me. You are my refuge. I don't know anything right now other than that. It's all I can hold on to right now, Lord."

The devastating end of my relationship with Michael sent me reeling. I had experienced rejection before, but this was different. Before I rededicated my life to the Lord, I always knew that I was taking a risk. I wasn't following God, I was in sin, and I knew there was a great possibility of it all ending in disaster. But this time around, I had tried so hard to do things the right way. I was seeking God with all my heart. I meant every single thing I said to the Lord. All I wanted was the best. I felt betrayed by Michael, but most of all, I felt betrayed by God. How could He do this to me? He knew all along that Michael was going to walk away from Nicholas and me, but He let me give my heart away nonetheless. I didn't understand it at all.

The following Wednesday night, I showed up at church as usual. I knew Michael would be there, so I had tried to prepare myself. What I didn't expect, though, was for him to show up with his new girlfriend. It seemed the joke was on me and I was the last to know. It was apparent that he had been seeing her for a while by how comfortable they were with each other. People had not told me what was going on because they were trying to protect me and didn't want me to be hurt. It was too late. I was crushed. I had been replaced yet again.

I cried for hours and hours that night, asking the same questions over and over. How could this have happened *again*? Was I destined for a life full of heartache and rejection? Was I cursed? Would I ever find someone who would be honest and committed to me?

CHAPTER 5

The Pain of Surrender

Each time I went to church, I had to see Michael and his new girlfriend together. About a month after we broke up, my pastor came to me one Sunday and told me that he had an announcement to make. I'll never forget his words to me. "Darlin'," he said, "I just want to give you a heads-up. I am announcing Michael's engagement to Brenda today. I thought you should hear it from me first. If you would like to leave, I'll understand."

I couldn't believe it. *Engagement?* Boy, he didn't waste any time, did he? I could feel my fighting spirit stirring within me and I was more determined than ever to rise to the occasion and not let them see me cry. As the announcement was made, I sat there rock solid. I didn't look around the room, but I could feel concerned eyes looking at me with sympathy. I bit my lip to keep it from quivering, but I made it through. I didn't back down and I didn't run away. I stood my ground.

MY JOURNEY TO THE HIGH PLACE OF PROMISE

That week the Lord dropped a book into my lap that caused a major turning point in my life. Years earlier, my dad had sent me a copy of *Hinds' Feet on High Places* by Hannah Hurnard. I had never taken the time to sit down and read it before, but during this season of pain and hardship, the Lord prompted me to pick it up.

Hinds' Feet on High Places is an allegory about a girl named Much-Afraid (appropriately so), a descendant of the Fearings, who lives in the Valley of Humiliation. Daily, Much-Afraid is tormented by her relatives, Craven Fear and Pride. One day, the Great Shepherd (Jesus) invites her to begin a journey to the High Places, out of the Valley of Humiliation and into His Father's kingdom, the Realm of Love. Along the way, the Great Shepherd promises to transform her crippled feet into "hinds' feet," ones that will enable her to move as painlessly and gracefully as a deer. He warns her that the journey will not be easy but gives her two companions—Sorrow and Suffering—to help her on her way. The Good Shepherd pledges to come to her aid if she calls and to protect her from any of her Fearing relatives.

Much-Afraid agrees to make the journey to the High Places with Sorrow and Suffering, but she encounters many times of hardship and trial along the way. After one particularly difficult battle, it seems she can see the High Places right in front of her and it appears as if she will arrive very soon.

Much-Afraid's story amazingly and accurately described my own. Jesus had called me on a journey to the High Places. Along the way, in my relationship with Michael, my goal (marriage) seemed so close, almost within arm's reach. But, like Much-Afraid's journey, the path was taking a turn.

One day the path turned a corner, and to her amazement and consternation she saw a great plain spread out beneath them. As far as the eye could see there seemed to be nothing but desert, and endless expanse of sand dunes, with not a tree in sight. . . . To the horror of Much-Afraid, her two guides [Sorrow and Suffering] prepared to take the steep path downward.

She stopped dead and said to them, "We mustn't go down there. The Shepherd has called me to the High Places. We must find some path which goes up, but certainly not down there." But they made signs to her that she was to follow them down the steep pathway to the desert below.

Much-Afraid looked to left and right, but though it seemed incredible, there was no way possible by which they could continue to climb upward. The hill they were on ended abruptly at this precipice, and the rocky cliffs towered above them in every direction straight as walls with no possible foothold.

"I can't go down there," panted Much-Afraid, sick with shock and fear. "He can never mean that—never! He called me up to the High Places, and this is an absolute contradiction of all that he promised."

As I read these words I remembered my own shock and fear on the day Michael called it quits. I thought it was impossible. Surely God couldn't have meant for Michael to reject me like that. I continued reading this story so like my own.

She then lifted up her voice and called desperately, "Shepherd, come to me. Oh, I need you, come and help me!"

In a moment he was there, standing beside her.

"Shepherd," she said despairingly, "I can't understand this. The guides you gave me say that we must go down there into that desert, turning right away from the High Places altogether. You don't mean that, do you? You can't contradict yourself. Tell them we are not to go there, and show us another way. Make a way for us, Shepherd, as you promised."

He looked at her and answered very gently, "That is the path, Much-Afraid, and you are to go down there."

"Oh, no," she cried. "You can't mean it. You said if I would trust you, you would bring me to the High Places, and that path leads right away from them. It contradicts all that you promised."

"No," said the Shepherd, "it is not contradiction, only *postponement for the best to become possible*."

Much-Afraid felt as though he had stabbed her to the heart. "You mean," she said incredulously, "you really mean that I am to follow that path down and down into the wilderness and then over that desert, away from the mountains indefinitely? Why," (and there was a sob of anguish in her voice) "it may be months, even years, before that path leads back to the mountains again. O Shepherd, do you mean it is indefinite postponement?"

My thoughts exactly. I felt as though God had stabbed me in the heart as well. And I realized it could be months, even years before I found the right man to make my family whole.

He bowed his head silently, and Much-Afraid sank on her knees at his feet, almost overwhelmed. *He was leading her away from her heart's desire altogether and gave no promise at all as to when he would bring her back*. As she looked out over what seemed an endless desert, the only path she could see led farther and farther away from the High Places, and it was all desert.

Then he answered very quietly, "Much-Afraid, do you love me enough to accept postponement and the *apparent* contradiction of the promise, and to go down there with me into the desert?"

She was still crouching at his feet, sobbing as if her heart would break, but now she looked up through her tears, caught his hand in hers, and said, trembling, "I do love you, you know that I love you. Oh forgive me because I can't help my tears. I will go down with you into the wilderness, right away from the promise, if you really wish it. Even if you cannot tell me why it has to be, I will go with you, for you know I do love you, and you have the right to choose for me anything that you please."[1]

I placed the book on the coffee table in front of me and closed my eyes. I knew what I had to do. I had been in desperate situations before and the Lord had always come to my rescue. But somehow, this time seemed different. God was asking me to turn away from my greatest heart's desire (to be married) and trust Him to fulfill His promise in *His timing*. I had to lay down my plans and expectations.

All along, I was doing everything God asked me to do because I believed He had a husband waiting for me just around the corner. But at this crossroads, I had to search the motives of my heart. Could I continue on the path He had for me without expecting a husband in return? Could I lay down everything that was precious to me and follow Him into the desert?

As I examined my heart and counted the cost, the Holy Spirit brought a story to my mind. I'd heard it many times over the years, though I haven't been able to find a printed copy of it anywhere.

A six-year-old girl was shopping with her mommy. They were almost finished running errands and had only one stop left before returning home. As they pulled into the parking lot of the local dollar store, the mom explained to her little girl that she was not there to buy toys, just to pick up a few things for their home. The little girl nodded emphatically, agreeing just to look and not to insist on buying any toys. But as much as the little girl tried to keep her promise, she was overwhelmed by all the beautiful toys.

One thing in particular stood out above all the rest of the items in the store, and when the little girl laid her eyes on it, she knew she would do whatever it took to get her mom to purchase it for her. It was a beautiful strand of plastic pearls, fit for a perfect little princess. The negotiations started, extra chores were promised, and by the time they arrived at the checkout, the girl's mom gave in to her desperate pleas.

For the next few months, this little girl wore her pearls proudly day in and day out. She wore them in the bathtub, she wore them on the playground, she wore them in Sunday school and she wore them to bed.

One night as her daddy tucked her into bed, he asked the little girl a question. "Honey, do you love me?"

The little girl answered, "Of course I do, Daddy!"

He smiled at her and looked at her pearls, which were beginning to look dull, even a little green around the edges. After a few moments, he asked her, "Would you be willing to give me your necklace?"

As she considered her father's question, the little girl began to panic. She couldn't think of any reason why her dad would want to take her precious pearls away. She was so fond of them, she couldn't imagine parting with them. Within moments, she had thought of a possible solution.

"I'll give you my favorite teddy, Daddy," she exclaimed, thinking that her bear was a sacrifice she could handle.

Her daddy smiled, kissed her on her forehead, and said, "That's okay, sweetheart, you can keep your teddy bear."

The next night, the girl's father came in again for prayers and a kiss good night. She was a bit nervous, wondering if he would ask her again to give up her beautiful strand of pearls. She quickly removed her pearls and hid them under her pillow.

Her dad leaned over and gently kissed her on the forehead, blessed her in prayer, and turned to leave her room. He stopped in the doorway, turned, and asked again, "Honey, do you love me?"

"Yes, Daddy," the little girl replied cautiously.

Her hand tightly grasped the strand of pearls hidden under her pillow as the dreaded question sounded again: "Will you give me your pearl necklace tonight?"

The little girl felt anger rising within her, and as a hot tear rolled down her face, she said, "I don't know where it is, Daddy. I must have lost it."

Again, he smiled kindly, walked toward her, and kissed her gently.

On the third night, the little girl had prepared herself for the inevitable. Her daddy walked in, but before he could say anything, she handed over the pearls.

Her daddy wiped the tears from her eyes and embraced her warmly. He reached in his pocket and pulled out a beautiful, black velvet box. The little girl watched with amazement as he opened the box, pulling out a brand-new strand of pearls. His eyes filled with tears as he said, "I was waiting for you to give me your old strand of plastic pearls so I could give you the real thing."

SURRENDER

For a whole night before His crucifixion, Jesus agonized in the Garden of Gethsemane. He sweat blood as He submitted His will to His Father.

I will never forget the pain of my own surrender. In moments such as these, our faith is deeply tested. Will we trust in

God's goodness to fulfill His promises to us? Will we truly let go, placing our lives fully in the hands of a loving Father?

August 30

Dear Jesus,

Thank You so much for putting Hinds' Feet in High Places in my lap at the exact time that I needed to read those encouraging words. I can relate so well to Much-Afraid and I'm excited to go with You to the High Places, no matter which direction the path follows. I do trust You that marriage is in my future, so until then just give me the grace to get through this time, making the most of every moment.

WHAT WILL YOU DO?

Have you been waiting for the right guy to come to your rescue? Driven by guilt and anxiety, are you searching for a father for your child? Do you feel a war of conflict in your mind and heart, struggling to make God your true Source? Let the Holy Spirit search your heart.

The Good Shepherd brings us all to moments of surrender. As I look back now, I am able to see how laying down my will enabled God to take me on paths I never dreamed possible.

ENDNOTES

1. Hannah Hurnard, *Hinds' Feet on High Places* (Wheaton, IL: Tyndale House Publishers, Inc., 1998), pp. 80–83, emphasis mine.

CHAPTER 6

Finding My Passion

The enemy almost succeeded in taking me out. I'm sure he must've celebrated on my day of defeat when I couldn't even muster up the desire to continue living. I can imagine how pleased he was that I blamed God for betraying me and hurting me. I can also picture his anger and rage when Jesus Himself came down and slammed the door of my heart in his face. The devil was humiliated and mocked when Jesus shouted at him, "That's enough. You must leave her alone now." Then He swooped down and filled me with an amazingly generous portion of grace. He took me, the vessel that had been emptied and drained, and began to shake me, allowing His grace to thoroughly fill me. This shaking process allowed my passions and gifts to rise to the surface.

Although I anticipated huge emotional and spiritual setbacks, it was incredible how swift the process of recovery was for me. I learned some valuable lessons as a result of this trial. In the world, when you make mistakes and fall flat on your face, you usually have to go back to the beginning and start all over again. People around you tend to judge you and lose faith in you. They will make you jump through every kind of hoop to make amends for what you did wrong. Fortunately for us, things are different in God's world. When you are living for God and walking on His path, when you mess up, you get up, shake it off, and learn from your mistake. Instead of going all the way back to the beginning, you go to the place where you had your last victory. With God, there is no jumping through hoops to make amends for what you did. There is simply a prayer of repentance and a request for forgiveness.

Applying the truth of God's Word, I was able to repent and turn back to God without wasting months in self-punishment. I dove into what God had for me, immersing myself in His Word. As a result, I soaked up amazing amounts of wisdom, knowledge, and revelation. Church and Christian conferences fueled my hunger for God, and the Lord faithfully met with me as I made myself available to Him.

I didn't have enough money to buy all the books I wanted to read and study, but my friends allowed me to borrow from their personal libraries. I devoured books month after month. Although I wasn't much of a reader in grade school and high school, I found myself craving understanding and instruction. (Between the time I got pregnant until Nicholas's second birthday, I had read well over 150 books.) I cultivated a spiritually rich environment in me and around me. In such a place, I could not help but grow and mature.

THE HEART OF AN INTERCESSOR

Although I still had needs and desires, I took on a new approach to receiving these things. Since God already knew what I needed, I decided to spend the majority of my time praying for the needs of others around me.[1] I learned later that this is the heart of a true intercessor. My prayer life exploded as I poured out my heart to God, especially concerning my family and friends.

Since the time I was a little girl, my mom struggled with alcoholism. I spent many nights in prayer for her, pleading with God to send His angels to protect her, heal her, and set her free. I also prayed for my friend Kim to be blessed. I labored in prayer for my little brother, who was lost and struggling with drug addiction. I agreed with my dad in prayer for the restoration of his marriage and his future ministry. Every time I felt discontent with my life, every time I felt a lack, I prayed for others. As I poured myself out in this way, God began to provide for me in unexpected and amazing ways.

DOING FOR OTHERS

Ever since Jesus rescued me, I knew God would use me to help other young women who were headed down the road I had already traveled. I always had a desire to help young women, and now there was a special place in my heart for single mothers. I told my pastor about my desire to help and he introduced me to a pregnant girl who was a few years younger than I was.

Lizzy had been pretty wild through her teenage years, but now she was returning to the Lord. I shared my testimony with her and felt instant compassion for her. I didn't know a lot, but I did know how to comfort someone who was pregnant and alone.

We enjoyed getting to know each other, sharing the hardships and joys of pregnancy. One night, I asked her what she was going to name the baby. She knew she was going to have a boy and had narrowed it down to two choices—Luke or Brandon. I told her I liked Luke and she mentioned she had been favoring that name as well. We discussed how names were important to God. Although I didn't know what Luke meant, I knew it was a strong biblical name.

I decided to give Lizzy a book titled *What to Expect When You're Expecting*.[2] My stepmom had sent it to me when she found out I was pregnant with Nicholas. But since I already had a copy, I thought I'd pass this one on to Lizzy.

When I started to hand it to her, a piece of paper fell to the floor. I picked it up and noticed it was a decorative certificate with the name Luke on it. Inscribed on the certificate was the meaning of the name and related Scriptures. Lizzy and I looked at each other, amazed and excited. I had never opened the book before that day, so we knew God was with us, blessing our time together—two single mothers meeting to encourage and love each other.

I want to emphasize how important it is to reach out to those around you. You may feel like you have nothing much to offer. You may not be an eloquent speaker or a gifted counselor. But God has commanded us to encourage one another. In fact, the best way to get your focus off of yourself is to put it on those around you. Do you know someone who is struggling? Is there a pregnancy center in your town where you can invest in other pregnant women? Who knows? Your testimony might help change a young girl's mind about abortion.

As I reached out and ministered to Lizzy, the Lord met us and opened up to me a whole new realm of purpose. For the first time in my life, I realized I had something to offer to others in need. I felt comforted knowing that even if I felt unqualified to help, I could ask the Holy Spirit to come.

God is strong in our weaknesses. If you are waiting to "get your act together" before you reach out and touch those around you, you might be waiting your whole life. God often uses in-experienced amateurs to do His best work.

September 30

Lord, I am Your passionate princess! I may not be perfect; in fact, I'm far from it. But there is one thing I know. You have set my feet upon the Rock and shown me the truth. I will forever be Your servant. I am a vessel You can use. I yield all I am and everything I have to You. My heart is 100 percent Yours. My goal in life is to serve You in any way I can. As long as You equip me with what I need, I will go where You tell me to go. I am learning to trust You in a way I never knew before. I love You with all my heart and I know that You are for me and not against me. I consider it an honor to be Yours.

PASSION, JOY, AND PURPOSE

My life was overflowing with joy. I was walking closely with God, I was recovering from the hurts of my past, and I was moving forward with hopes and dreams of ministering to young women. I loved my little Nicholas and God was faithfully providing spiritual families who took us in and loved us like we were their own. I was receiving new understanding about God and was connecting often with other single moms in need.

By pouring my energy into all these activities and relationships, I built a wall of stability around me. Finding my purpose and catching God's vision for my life was my key to happiness. I no longer struggled through depression, dwelling on my loneliness, my singleness, or my financial worries.

Every single mom should pursue God's vision and purpose for her life. Do not overschedule yourself simply to escape your problems. Find your passions, the things that inspire you, and fill your life with those things.

October 10

God, I will never turn away from You. You have placed a hunger inside me and it is great. You have saved my life and given me a purpose and a vision. That means the world to me. I have felt Your perfect mercy, and Your grace has consumed me. When I have been weak, You are strong. You have been so faithful to me. I can feel myself growing every day and I'm so thankful that I didn't have to start all over after what happened with Michael. I love You, Lord!

PARENTING

Nicholas was another passion of mine. The Lord taught me much about being a good mom. In fact, He's still teaching me ways to cultivate a good relationship with Nicholas. I learned that there is a perfect balance between my life of ministry and purpose and my life as a mother meeting the needs of her child. He showed me that my role as a mother was to create an environment for my son where God the Father was represented in a loving way so when he was ready to spread his wings and leave the nest, he would have a solid bond and growing relationship with his heavenly Father.

FOUNDATIONS

The Trinity—God the Father, Jesus the Son, and the Holy Spirit—parallels our family structure here on earth. In Genesis 1:26, God said, "Let us make man in Our image, according to Our likeness." God the Father is the head of the family of God.

The Holy Spirit, a nurturer who is also called the Comforter, takes on the role of mother. Jesus is the firstborn Son.

Any negative family experiences—whether it be with your father, mother, or siblings—can greatly affect how you relate to the three members of the Trinity. For example, if you had an abusive father, you may struggle to love and trust God the Father. It is vital for you to walk through the steps of inner healing (emphasized in chapter two) so that you can feel safe and loved by the entire triune God. Then you will be able to correctly represent God to your children.

THE WAR AGAINST THE FAMILY STRUCTURE

Throughout time, Satan has waged a war against the family structure. Within the past few decades, it seems he has specifically targeted the American culture. In our country, single parents run 11.9 million families, an increase of 73 percent since 1980. Single mothers—divorced, widowed, or never married—account for some 9.8 million of that total.[3] To me, that's too many to be a coincidence. In Malachi 4:6, the Lord says He is going to "turn the hearts of the fathers to the children, and the hearts of the children to their fathers." Now, why would God have to do that unless there had been a definite separation between the two?

If the enemy can succeed in keeping children alienated from their earthly fathers, they will more than likely grow up suspicious of their heavenly Father as well. But God does not expose the enemy's strategies without offering hope and a plan of victory. He has given me some great tools to share with single mothers everywhere in order to bring restoration to their children. My ultimate vision (as well as God's) is to see Malachi 4:6 take place. But until that time, we will rise above the war against family structure and emerge victorious through God's grace.

FAMILY FIRST

Tool number one was the realization that Nicholas was my *first* ministry. I had to embrace the fact that no matter how much opportunity waited for me to minister to others, Nicholas needed me the most. The Holy Spirit revealed to me that the Lord would never require me to minister to someone else at the expense of my child.

I also learned that, at times, my baby took away from time I could spend alone with God. At first it didn't seem very "holy" to spend most of my evening bathing and feeding my toddler. Condemnation came over me—"You're not praying enough, you're not reading the Word enough"—until I heard the Lord whisper to my heart that by spending time with Nicholas and taking care of him, I was also spending time with God. It blesses Him when we serve our children. There is a special "allowance" for mothers who don't get a lot of alone time with God. He knows why you are not able, and He is pleased with your dedication.

DISCIPLINE

Tool number two was to not let guilt dictate the way I disciplined my child. We can't tiptoe around being firm with our little ones because of any guilt we may feel that a father figure is not around. Without discipline, we keep our children from being fully prepared for society. I suggest finding a couple in your church who have well-behaved, well-adjusted kids. Ask them if they can share wisdom with you and mentor you in the area of parenting.

Discipline stems from the word *disciple*. As mothers, it is important that we disciple our little ones into their destinies with wisdom and grace.

LITTLE GIRLS, GOD'S PRINCESSES

Despite the fact that I don't have a daughter, through the years the Lord has given me great insight as to how single mothers can raise up their little girls to be great women of God. Since girls mature more quickly than boys, it's appropriate to dialogue with them about God at a very young age, even before the age of two.

Girls have been wired by God to have three basic needs.

1. A young girl needs to feel lovely, desirable, cherished, and valued. She needs to grow up knowing that she is worth fighting for.
2. She needs to feel safe. She needs to know that her daddy is strong enough to protect her.
3. She needs to know that she has greatness in her and that she was created for an important purpose. She needs to believe that the world is a better place because she was born.

If these needs are not met at home when a girl is young, she will go out in the world in search of them. She will search high and low, most likely settling for something that feels close.

For example, she might mistake a young boy's lust as the solution to her need to be desired and cherished. When she discovers he desires her not for who she is, but for what she has to give, she will be devastated.

To satisfy her need to feel protected, she might feel attracted to a selfish, controlling bully of a man. At first his apparent strength will draw her and impress her. But if she does something he doesn't like, she will quickly find out he is not her protector; rather, she is his victim.

So how can you, as a mother, prevent these things from happening?

The first and most important step is prayer. After a few years of raising Nicholas, the Lord showed me a vision that released me from any guilt or worry I was carrying concerning the awesome weight of single motherhood. In my quiet time with God one evening, I saw a surface that was jagged and rough. Then a pitcher that was filled with some kind of gel appeared and poured over it. When the pitcher was empty, the gel settled into all the cracks and crevices, and when it dried, the surface was perfectly smooth. The Holy Spirit told me that the surface represented my child and what he had endured from being born into an incomplete family. The Lord was right there, however, and the gel was His soothing grace, covering any flaws or imperfections. His grace was all consuming and all changing, and it made the jagged surface perfectly smooth.

God's grace is available to all of us; especially, I believe, for single mothers and their children.

As you continue in prayer, ask the Lord to supernaturally meet those needs in your little girl. Ask Him to make her feel desired, beautiful, cherished, safe, and protected. Make this the cry of your heart. As she grows, tell her about God. Tell her how He is her Daddy, and explain that His job is to protect her heart. Portray Him as the Hero of her heart and remind her of how much He cherishes her.

Next (and you can pray about the right age for this), introduce her to the Lord personally. Explain to your little one that God is always talking to us, but He doesn't always speak our language. Lots of times He speaks in other ways, like through pictures in our minds, songs, stories, or dreams.

Tell your child to close her eyes and picture a big tree. When she can visualize it, explain to her that God is going to visit her. Ask her to tell you what she sees, hears, smells, etc. Then ask

Jesus to show Himself to you both. When Jesus comes (and He will), ask your daughter if she has any questions to ask Him. Ask her what Jesus looks like. Invite her to sit in Jesus' lap. Ask Jesus to take her to the Father.

During this experience, pay close attention to what your child tells you. You may have to ask a lot of questions because some kids won't give you details without being prompted. At the same time, ask the Holy Spirit what He'd like to do and what direction He'd like to go in.

It may take a few sessions to feel comfortable with this process. The first time I did it with Nicholas, it blew me away. I thought, *Everyone should be doing this with their kids! If I had seen the Lord like this when I was little, how much would that have changed my life?* I suggest doing it on a weekly basis. As your children get older, encourage them to do it whenever they want, even when you're not around. They can meet the Lord personally whenever they choose. It's an amazing tool for them to have.[4]

LITTLE BOYS, PRINCES OF GOD

Now let's talk about boys. God seems to have wired them with one main question in their hearts: "Do I have what it takes to succeed, to win?" This question applies to being a man of God, a good son, a good husband, a good father, and a man of strength and integrity.

If a boy doesn't get this question answered at home, at a young age, it will send him on a quest to find out if he "has what it takes." He might find the woman of his dreams and elevate her to the place God is supposed to hold in his life. She becomes his source of encouragement, his source of identity, and his source of accomplishment.

Another way he may do this is by acquiring badges of achievement that he can wear on his shirt like medals of honor. He may spend his entire life climbing the ladder of success, searching for approval from others. However, all his achievements and efforts will not fill the emptiness in his heart because his worth will be wrapped up in what he can *do*, not who he *is*.

Another thing to be cautious about with our little men is their strong tendency to want to protect Mom. It's okay for them to do that to a certain degree, but it's important for them to know that Mom believes God protects her. If boys are raised to understand this, they won't try to carry a burden that is impossible for them. It will also make a significant difference when it comes time for Mom to get married. The son won't fight so hard to be the head of the household with the potential husband if he understands that God already holds the Father position.

The spiritual process with boys is much the same as with girls—prayer, introduction of God through stories, and then leading into personal encounters—but, the *emphasis* will be different. Focus on how proud God is of His son, how confident the Lord is that your boy has what it takes.

A MAN'S INVOLVEMENT

As boys and girls get older, I think it's important for mothers to look for trustworthy men, either in the church or in the family, to spend time with their children. You will want to communicate clearly that you're not looking for a father for them, only a male leader and friend. Sometimes men are more than willing to help a single mom in this way, but they are afraid of her motives and expectations. If you initiate open communication, that may help the men around you to not feel pressured and they may open up tremendously to your children as a result.

Sometimes God will supernaturally send the right men your way, and other times you'll have to pray them in, searching earnestly for the right people. If there is no one who qualifies, don't worry. Remember the grace God has for you and your kids. Don't get so desperate for male leadership that you settle for someone who doesn't have the qualities you want your child to emulate.

If we follow these guidelines and ask the Holy Spirit for a plan that is custom made for each child, I believe we will raise amazing men and women of God!

A CALL TO THE CHURCH

My mission is to bring the church to a new awareness of the needs of single mothers. Join with me in prayer on this endeavor. I believe we are on the brink of seeing great compassion from the body of Christ for single mothers and their children. You may feel like your church doesn't reach out to you enough. Make it the cry of your heart that your needs and the needs of your children would be known. It's only a matter of time before we see breakthrough in this area.

FINDING YOUR PURPOSE AND CALL

Some of you might feel a bit lost, wondering exactly how to find your purpose and calling. Here are some steps to take as you begin your search.

1. **REFLECTION.** Most of us, if we stepped back and took a closer look at our lives, would see a clear calling. Set aside some time and reflect on the following questions:

    - What are your natural gifts, talents, and abilities?
    - What do you long to do or accomplish?

- What prophetic words have you received that may indicate God's plan for you?
- What dreams has God given you about your future?
- If money and time were no object, what would you do with your life?

2. **PRAYER.** Take all your requests and uncertainties to God in prayer. Be sure to listen to what He has to say to you. Write down Scriptures that speak to you.

3. **RESEARCH.** Interview those who know you best—your parents, siblings, friends, and mentors. Ask them what they see in you, areas in life where you excel, etc. This is very helpful because sometimes we have trouble seeing the obvious work that God is doing in us.

After you take some time to consider these questions, you might have a clearer idea of where you can invest yourself and your time. I have found it particularly helpful to write things down in a journal. Not only do I have a record of my thoughts and prayers, but I am able to process them as I express them on paper.

October 20

Jesus, tonight I come to You because my heart is full of anticipation. I feel like You are showing me pieces of the puzzle that is my life. I feel like the struggles in my life up to this point have equipped me with the tools I need to fulfill my destiny. I feel like You have shown me what my ministry will be. God, I feel in my heart that You have called me to minister to young women in order to save them from the same snares that I fell into. You have already put many things in my heart to share with them. Help me to find effective ways to do it.

FULFILLING YOUR DESTINY

1. **PLAN.** Start planning now by setting goals. After going through the exercises above, you should have a better idea of what you desire for your future.

2. **ATMOSPHERE.** Create an atmosphere in which you can succeed. For example, if you desire to work with troubled teens, you cannot stay at home and wait for teens to show up at your door! Get out there and find the places where you can make a start. Tell your pastor and friends about your desires and how you would like to be involved. Search for organizations that are doing what you desire to do. In the above case, something like Teen Challenge might be a good place to start.

3. **MENTOR.** Find people who are successfully doing what you desire to do. Ask them how they got there and if they have any advice to share.

4. **PRAYER.** Seal all your plans in prayer. Open your heart to God. Let Him know that you want to be used by Him. Ask Him to open the right doors and close the wrong ones, to guide you in the direction that He would have you go.

ENDNOTES

1. Don't get me wrong. God wants us to present our requests to Him. He says in James 4:2, "You do not have because you do not ask." However, during this season of my life, God was teaching me to focus on others instead of myself.

2. Heidi Murkoff, *What to Expect When You're Expecting* (Workman Publishing Company, third edition published in 2002).

3. This statistic came from www.businessweek.com, January 2005.

4. Not only is this a special way to help your children connect to God in a personal way, it is a great tool for adults as well. Many people disregard such experiences, claiming they are based solely on one's "imagination." I believe God created our imaginations, and He did so with the intent of using them to communicate with us.

CHAPTER 7

The Story of Ruth

From the time I discovered I was pregnant, I struggled to make ends meet. For single mothers, money represents survival. I had to learn how to trust and depend on the Lord to meet my needs in many ways, especially with my bills. One realization that every single mother comes to at some point is that if she can trust God with her money issues, she can trust Him in *any* situation.

Money is very important to God.

THE TITHE

In the kingdom of God, tithing—giving 10 percent of our earnings to the church—is a principle that forms the foundation of all financial and spiritual blessings. When I was growing up, I knew my parents gave money to the church, but I had no idea that the Lord commanded it as a symbol of our obedience and trust in Him. At first, it proved difficult for me to make this sacrifice. There were weeks when money was so tight that I was forced to decide between tithing and filling up my car with gas or buying diapers for Nicholas.

I didn't realize that God wanted to increase my faith. He wanted an opportunity to show off, to be the One to swoop in on an impossible situation and miraculously provide what was desperately needed. Every time I withheld my tithe and tried to work things out in my own strength, I robbed God of an opportunity to bless me and heroically save the day.

Malachi 3:10 states:

> Bring all the tithes into the storehouse, that there may be food in My house, and try Me now in this," says the Lord of hosts, "if I will not open for you the windows of heaven and pour out for you such blessing that there will not be room enough to receive it.

After reading this promise, I made a covenant with God to tithe. Why not take the chance and give Him the opportunity to prove His faithfulness to me? To this very day, He has never let me down.

November 1

God, sometimes I feel resentful because of my financial situation. I've been working hard for everything since I was in high school, paying my own way. But now I don't have any money. I receive no welfare, no child support, and no rental assistance. The only thing I get is WIC for Nicholas's formula, and they remind me every month that their program is not designed to provide all the food for my baby, just some.

God, I'm sorry I haven't tithed. Will You please help me to do that? Give me the strength and the faith it takes to trust in You for my provision. Help me to pay my bills on time, and help me to spend my money appropriately. Help me not to get discouraged by my financial situation. Remind me that money problems can be solved easily.

Father, I pray that You will help me stay focused on You and not my bills. Provide a way for them to be taken care of. I don't believe that it is Your will for my bills to go unpaid. I believe You want to bless my socks off. I don't know how or when, but I get butterflies inside when I think about what kind of miracle You're going to do. I will wait on You.

God, thank You so much for always coming through for me, just in time! You know what my needs are for the week coming up. If You don't supply the money somehow, then please give me a plan as to what to do with my bills. You take control, God. I hand it all over to you.

TESTIMONIES OF GOD'S PROVISION

After I fully grasped the concept of tithing, some truly amazing things started happening.

One day, while doing laundry, I thought, *Nicholas needs socks, but I don't have any money right now to buy any.* I didn't pray about it or even put it into words; I just had a passing thought. The next Sunday, when I went to church, there was a bucket of baby socks with a tag on it that said, "To Nicholas, From Someone Who Cares." Whoever it was, that "Someone Who Cares" had heard directly from God about what I needed for Nicholas. The same thing happened with Easter outfits, shoes, diapers, all kinds of things. I was amazed time after time when I had a need and I would show up at church to find the need had been met. I never did find out for sure who "Someone Who Cares" was. But I know God is blessing that person for his or her obedience.

I heard some people in my church pray for checks to come in the mail. At first I thought that was silly, but I tried it for myself, and guess what? Once, when I was in a pinch, I received $350 and I was able to pay all my bills. Another time it was $500. I still pray for God to surprise me with checks in the mail. And He still does! It is such a treat to go to the mailbox and open an envelope containing money.

Another day, I worried about the fact that I had no baby food. Payday was still a couple of days away, and I thought about who I could ask for money. That evening when I got home from work, my roommate said, "There was a really good sale on baby food today, so I picked some up for you." My jaw dropped in disbelief. She had never done anything like that before and never did anything like it since.

Another time, I ran low on baby food (again) and I went to church that evening with the weight of that burden on my heart, praying that God would come through for me. Wanda, one of the women in my church, came up to me and told me she had something for me. I walked out to her car with her and she had a whole tub full of baby food. I cried, thanking her for the gift. God had heard my prayer again, and He used a friend in the church to meet my need.

Many times when I was pumping gas at the station, I would cringe thinking about the money I was spending. On several occasions, someone from the church would pull into the gas station and offer to pay for my gas.

After I had lost all my pregnancy weight, my clothes were too big for me, but I had no money to do anything about it. I prayed about it all week, asking God to bless me with new clothes. That Sunday at church, my pastor gave me his credit card and told me to go to the mall and get some new clothes. Now, how many pastors do you know who would do something like that? It seemed like every time I turned around, God was proving His ability to provide for me.

However, even in the midst of many financial miracles, I still doubted and wondered about the stability of my future. I couldn't help it. No matter how many times God proved faithful, it was always scary for me when money ran out. But, as time when on, I opened myself up more and became more vulnerable before God. I no longer tried to be tough and self-sufficient, doing it all on my own, but threw myself into the hands of my Provider. Being vulnerable was scary, but it was worth it!

LAY IT ON ME

Over a period of a few weeks, I felt the Lord urging me to study the book of Ruth. I had no knowledge of this story other than that it was in the Bible. One day when I was spending time with Barb, I asked her, "If you could compare me to anyone in the Bible, who would it be?" She thought about it briefly before answering, "Ruth." I took her answer as a confirmation to begin a study of the book of Ruth.

As I read, I was blessed, but I didn't completely understand how it all fit into my life until I found a book written by Perry Stone Jr., a pastor and founder of Voice of Evangelism Ministries in Cleveland, Tennessee. It was called *Lay It On Me: Discover the Hidden Truths in the Book of Ruth that Will Enable You to Move into God's Ultimate Plan and Blessing*. The parallels I found between my life and the life of Ruth blew me away. With every page I read, I became more and more excited.

THE STORY OF RUTH

The story of Ruth is amazing and romantic. It begins with a woman named Naomi. Naomi was a Jew, a godly woman raised in Bethlehem. Due to a famine, Naomi's husband decided to uproot his family and travel to Moab, a land of idol worship across the Jordan River. Naomi's two sons married women from Moab. Tragedy gripped the family. Naomi's husband and two sons died within ten years of their arrival in Moab. There remained just the three widows—Naomi, Orpah, and Ruth.

After the death of her husband and sons, Naomi received reports that the famine had ended in Bethlehem. Embittered by the hardships and heartbreak she had suffered in Moab, she planned a return to her homeland.

When Naomi informed her daughters-in-law of her plan to return to Bethlehem, they both pledged to go with her. Naomi urged them to stay in their own land so they could remarry and remain close to their families and in their own culture. After some debate, Orpah kissed her mother-in-law good-bye and returned to the house of her family. But Ruth refused to leave Naomi's side. She was willing to leave everything she had ever known—friends, family, even her own religion and culture—to follow Naomi to Bethlehem.

Ruth's response to Naomi's request was poetic. She said:

Entreat me not to leave you, or to turn back from following after you; for wherever you go, I will go; and wherever you lodge, I will lodge; your people shall be my people, and your God, my God. Where you die, I will die, and there will I be buried. The Lord do so to me, and more also, if anything but death parts you and me.[1]

Orpah and Ruth represent two types of people in the church today. There are those who flirt with the idea of serving God and going wherever He's called them (Orpahs) and those who are loyal and faithful, serving the Lord no matter what the cost (Ruths).

Before my pregnancy, my life was a sad version of Orpah's. I made many promises to God, but never followed through on them. I told Him countless times, "Someday I'll serve you, God, but right now I just want to have fun." After my transformation and renewed commitment to Christ, I saw how God's grace had made me like Ruth: loyal and faithful despite difficulty and hardship.

Ruth knew that Moab represented death. She knew there was nothing there for her anymore, just as I knew there was nothing for me back home. We both had received an invitation to step out in faith and travel to a place where we could start afresh.

Many people stay in "Moab" because it feels familiar and comfortable. But in order to receive everything God has for you, you may be required to come out of your place of comfort. It's not always an easy decision. I struggled for weeks with the thought of leaving all my family and friends. I had a lot of doubts and fears. But I also sensed a special opportunity. I, like Ruth, decided to follow my heart.

GLEANING: THE FIRST LEVEL OF BLESSING

Upon their arrival in Bethlehem, Ruth experienced very humble beginnings. Jewish law required landowners to leave certain areas of their fields unharvested so that the widows, the poor, and foreigners could glean grain to survive. Ruth took advantage of this opportunity and worked hard from morning until evening, gathering grain for herself and Naomi. Although many of the female workers took breaks throughout their day to visit and rest, Ruth did not. As a result of her hard work, she gained the attention and favor of the landowner, Boaz.

At I reflected on the story, I realized that Boaz represented Jesus in my life. I imagined Jesus noticing as I strolled into Tennessee, looking for a way to survive. I imagined Him watching me as I focused on "laboring faithfully in the fields" by studying and spending hours in prayer and in church (not to mention working full time as a waitress for "meager" wages).

At first, I couldn't figure out how Naomi fit into my life, but then it came to me. Just as Ruth stood by Naomi's side to minister to her and take care of her, considering herself to be the last priority, I was doing the same thing for my child! I could see how I had found favor in the eyes of Boaz (Jesus).

Are you laboring faithfully in the assignment God has given you, or are you constantly distracted by wishing you were in a better field? In his book, Stone writes, "Most of the time, it may seem your labor goes unnoticed and your efforts unrewarded." Many single mothers experience such humble beginnings. He continues: "You may be isolated in the corner of the harvest field where it feels like no one is paying attention. Yet, you are working, striving, not for attention, but because you have an assignment from God." While you slave away, it is easy to forget that your Boaz (Jesus), "sees you in the corner. He is providing for you because you are in HIS field!" Take heart! This level of gleaning is only the first level of blessing. "You will not always be in the corner by yourself working for someone else!"[2]

BOAZ

So, who *is* this Boaz? He was not only a wealthy businessman living in Bethlehem. He was also a close relative of Naomi's.

When I realized this, I switched modes and saw that Boaz, in addition to representing Jesus, might possibly also represent my future husband. My heart started skipping beats as I anticipated a love story.

Have you ever heard the expression "Timing is everything"? How about, "It's not what you know, it's who you know"? Who could have guessed that as Ruth unselfishly dropped everything to serve Naomi, Naomi would be the key to bringing in Ruth's miracle? I recalled all the connections I had made in Tennessee. As I walked in God's will, a confidence came over me that my divine appointments were being lined up as well. After all, God is the one who told me to study Ruth's life!

INCREASE: THE SECOND LEVEL OF BLESSING

As Ruth continued in her daily routine, she unknowingly stepped into her second level of blessing. Boaz took his field guards aside and instructed them to follow Ruth and throw extra portions of grain her way when she wasn't looking. Stone notes: "It was a sign of favor. The 'boss' was recognizing her for her hard work and the commitment she had made. She didn't ask for the additional grain but she got it any way. Boaz was blessing her on purpose!"[3]

Although this second level of blessing was not Ruth's final destination, it was a marked increase from her days of gleaning. "Prior to this, she had just enough. Now she had 'enough and then some!'"[4] This principle reveals the will of God for the single mother. Our God is a God of increase and promotion.

Upon seeing the favor that Ruth was receiving from Boaz, Naomi realized there could be a possible love connection, so she began to devise a plan to hook these two up.

THE THRESHING FLOOR

During the season of harvest, wheat would be piled up at the threshing floor. At night, when the wind picked up, the wheat separated from the chaff. In this story, the separation of the wheat and the chaff is symbolic of the way God separates the good from the bad in our lives. He "sifts" us, if you will.

I've heard it preached that you might have a breakdown before you get your breakthrough. Throughout our spiritual journeys, it seems as if God often lets us go through the storm before we are allowed to see the rainbow. This enables God to be strong in us when we are weak, and it gives Him an opportunity to build our character and integrity.

Landowners often slept at the threshing floor to guard their harvest from robbers. Naomi decided this would be the ideal place for Ruth to approach Boaz to let him know she was "available." This was a risky thing for Ruth to do because Boaz could reject her. God was calling her to step out in faith once again. Would she answer a second time with courage and obedience?

> The separation of the wheat from the chaff occurs at night when the wind blows and the darkness has settled around you. You cannot discern what is happening at the time, but those small storms and long nights alone are removing the impurities from you so the fruit of the spirit can come forth (Galatians 5:22–23). Boaz (Jesus) must separate the good from the bad, the wheat from the chaff in order to bring you to the [third level of blessing]! We must take a trip to the threshing floor in order to become everything God intended us to be. The chaff could be pride, rebellion, or stubbornness. It could represent one thing that, if it surfaced down the road, could ruin your family, your life, or your ministry.
>
> Before God uses you on a large scale . . . there will be some nights on the winnowing floor! . . . All spiritual testing is designed to sift your faith . . . .
>
> Midnight is the turning point. Changes occur at midnight. . . . As darkness settled over Bethlehem and the full moon hung over the rugged Judean mountains, Ruth quietly made her way toward the threshing floor. As she stealthily approached Boaz, she knelt and uncovered his feet. It appears he didn't realize she was there for some time. Have you ever prayed and felt like God was paying you no attention?[5]
>
> Although Ruth was in intense discomfort about becoming completely vulnerable with Boaz, she obeyed Naomi's advice. She was able to maintain a level of grace and dignity and she didn't panic.

God soon answered her prayer. Boaz took Ruth as his bride. Because she was a woman of "noble character,"[6] she found favor in the eyes of God and man.

PROVISION: THE THIRD LEVEL OF BLESSING

In the blink of an eye, Ruth's entire world changed. She stepped into her third level of blessing: total provision. When Boaz married Ruth, she was instantly elevated to a position of great prominence and influence in Bethlehem. She was now walking in the highest level of blessing.

Perry describes it this way:

> It is the realm of increase where your "cup is running over" (Psalm 23:5). . . . It was all a divine setup. It was a prearranged God moment. . . . When you are talented and dedicated to God, you will gain the attention of many . . . [but] you must stay in the area that God has placed you until the end of the mission. An early departure may result in an aborted destiny . . . .

> Ruth received instructions well. She knew how to listen to those who had experience in their realm of expertise. . . . It is imperative for us to be in the right place at the right time! Ruth saw potential for increase. If she moved to another field, she would have to go back to gleaning in a corner again.[7]

CONNECTION

I connected with Ruth from the very beginning. When I started out in Tennessee, I had "just enough." At a point like this, many women lose hope and give up. But, as I learned from Ruth, I took heart, knowing that my labor and perseverance would attract the favor of heaven. I was so encouraged I thought, *Oh! This is just the first level! That means I am going to be promoted from this place!*

Knowing that promotion was in my future, I was filled with strength to endure my season of gleaning. It's as if I sat back, took a deep breath and relaxed. I "chilled out," knowing my lack would not last forever. Better times were on the way!

As I witnessed Ruth reach her second level, I soaked it all in, paying close attention so I did not miss out on moving to *my* next level. I often daydreamed about how it was all going to happen. Would I catch the eye of some businessman who was looking for a dynamic young woman eager to be financially successful? Would I marry into a wealthy situation? Would it all just be given to me? I didn't know, and I really didn't care. I just thought it was cool that something bigger was in store.

God taught me that *blessing* does not always mean money. During this time, I realized that I had certain ideas of what *blessing* signified. God showed me that His blessings come in many different ways and forms. I began to treasure not only my financial breakthroughs, but also my spiritual and emotional growth.

I hope that while reading this biblical Cinderella story, you had an "Aha!" moment. I know I did. As I read Stone's spin on the story of Ruth, it was as if a light bulb went off in my head. I was astonished to see how closely my life paralleled Ruth's story of blessing.

REACH YOUR NEW LEVELS

As a single mom struggling to keep afloat, think about the story of Ruth. Study her life and hear God speak His precious promises to you. When you are faithful, God takes notice. Ask for grace to continue working hard and to recognize your blessing when it comes. God will use people to bless you or connect you along the way. (If we could see behind the scenes, we would probably be amazed at how much influence the Holy Spirit has on other people's hearts, causing them to give to us and grant us favor).

As you trust God with your future, and specifically for financial blessing, apply these important principles to your life:

1. Tithe. This is not just a good idea; it is a decision that will bring you much closer to the Lord. Challenge God's offer and test Him in this area. Open the door for financial miracles and provision in your life.
2. Be teachable and faithful. Such attitudes grab God's attention and move Him to pour out blessings on you.
3. Remember, timing is everything. It's not only a matter of being able to wait for God to move; it's your attitude during the wait that determines your level of blessing.

ENDNOTES

1. Ruth 1:16–17.
2. Perry Stone Jr., *Lay It On Me: Discover the Hidden Truths in the Book of Ruth that Will Enable You to Move into God's Ultimate Plan and Blessing* (Cleveland, TN: Voice of Evangelism Ministries, Inc., 1998), p. 43.
3. Ibid., p. 47.
4. Ibid., p. 49.
5. Ibid., pp. 58–63.
6. Ruth 3:11 (NIV).
7. Stone, pp. 51–54.

CHAPTER 8

Feeling God's Love

Up until this point in my life, I had experienced God in many ways. During my pregnancy, He was my Hero; as I dealt with my past mistakes, He was my Healer and Restorer. He was a safe Father. When I fell on my face He picked me up and became my Encourager and Friend. But I had yet to come to know Him as my intimate Lover.

Ever since I was a young child, I'd heard the words "God loves you," but it wasn't as real to me as I wanted it to be. I knew it in my mind but I couldn't feel it enough to be satisfied in my heart.

You've probably heard it said that love is a verb, an action. But love is also a feeling. What good does it do for someone to act love out to you if you can't feel it in return?

I had experienced brief encounters of the intimate love of God, but I was finding it difficult to *abide* in that love. When the moment passed and the feeling faded, I began to waiver. Whispers of doubt echoed in my ears, and pretty soon I felt depressed and thought I was alone in the world, hidden from God.

I am a passionate person. Many times after Nicholas was born, I craved physical attention so intensely that I felt I would crawl out of my skin. The enemy tried hard to isolate me during this time, bombarding me with thoughts and ideas of a distant God. But Jesus was beckoning my heart, stirring a desire within me to experience a baptism of His love. It was a step of faith. He was asking me to take a chance on Him.

December 6

Dear Jesus,

I wanted to spend some time with You tonight. As I was reading Six Hours One Friday by Max Cucado, I felt this incredible urge to know You better. I couldn't help but wish I had lived when You did. If I would have met You, I would've latched on to You and never left Your side. I can see myself giving up a life of marriage, children, anything conventional, just to follow You and observe Your mighty ways.

So then I got to thinking, I can still do that. I believe with all my heart and soul that You could make Yourself so real to me that a human body would be no more tangible to me than You, my Lord.

I want what the disciples had. I want to be as close to You as they were. I want You to make Yourself as real to me as You were to them when You walked beside them every day. If You show me how to have this kind of relationship with You, I mean really show me, then I will do everything I can to know You well. You know me better than I know myself, so it's only fair that I get to know You as much!

At this point, all I know to do is ask for what I desire. From what I've learned about You so far, I know You want me to desire You more.

Now, I can't guarantee that I'll feel that way every day, but Jesus, You understand what it's like to deal with fleshly desires. You may not have birthed a child, but You endured physical torture and pain when You were crucified. And You may not have ever joined Yourself intimately with a woman and then had her betray You, cheat on You, and lie to You. But one of your closest friends denied You, not once, but three times.

So I guess it's time the enemy forgot the idea that he can convince me that because I'm a woman and You walked this earth as a man, You don't understand the pain I've suffered. Self-pity has really been trying to get to me and I won't take it anymore. It will leave me alone, in the name of Jesus Christ! My enemy will not win. I will never again let my enemy and his slimy sidekicks rule my life. They have lost their battle when it comes to this woman! Not only am I saved through the mighty blood of Jesus, but I am dedicating my entire life to defeating the enemy in as many other lives as possible.

God, I pray that You will train me and lead me in the right direction to be a mighty warrior in Your kingdom. This son of mine is also going to be Yours. I promise I will do everything in my power to teach him about You and what You stand for.

I believe that if I just have faith, You will reveal Yourself to me.

MY MISCONCEPTIONS OF LOVE

In my quest for deeper levels of intimacy with the Lord, I had to overcome my misconceptions of love. Because of my past experiences, I had narrow ideas and unrealistic expectations of what love was, and I didn't know how to receive God's pure, perfect love. Without knowing it, I had created limits for God.

I expected Him to love me as a man could love me. I had basically put God in a box . . . a very small box.

God did not meet my needs the way I asked Him to or expected Him to. Instead, He opened my eyes to show me a new reality. His reality. During my season of single motherhood, the greatest thing God did for me was expand my mind to possibilities I had never imagined or considered. God is so creative! He has many different ways of reaching us. I had to let Him out of the box in which I had placed Him and let Him express His love for me however He chose.

Let God out of the box you have built. Don't limit Him. Let Him express His love for you however and whenever He chooses. Don't try to make it happen and don't put time restrictions on Him. Just be available for Him. He wants to be active in your life and pour out His love on you. Expect amazing experiences with Him, but don't expect to know how or when it's going to happen.

God loves the underdog! There is something about a woman in need that moves the heart of God.

God's heart is the single mother's advocate. We see this principle over and over in the Bible. The Scripture gives several instructions to take care of those in need: the widows (single moms), the orphans, the poor, the sick, those who are in bondage, and those who are hurting.

LOVE ENCOUNTERS

One weekday, Nicholas was sick and I stayed home from work to take care of him. I felt burdened that day, so I sat down and poured out my heart to God.

February 10

I'm really tired and worn out today, Lord. Life seems to be getting the best of me. I am trying to hold my head up, but it's hard. Everything in me tells me that something big is supposed to happen soon. Every book I read, every sermon I hear, every Scripture I read, and every song I sing speaks of this.

I wonder if I'm the only one who feels this way. Do we all have to go through the wine press in order to experience Your blessing?

I try not to question what You are doing in my life, or even Your timing, but I am afraid. I could easily get excited about my future. I have had dreams, visions, prophetic words, and notions that You are getting ready to send me a breakthrough. But there is a big part of me that doesn't want to hold on to this hope, just in case it isn't real. It seems like whenever I've gotten really excited about something in life and I've grabbed on to it, it's been ripped away from me. I end up feeling devastated. So what do I do?

I am so confused, Lord. Does this hesitance mean I don't have faith? If that's what it is, then please, give me faith! I'm not demanding that You hurry up with what You have planned for me. I'm just asking for Your reassurance that You haven't forgotten me.

Here are my dreams, Lord. Here are the desires of my heart. I first want to get so close to You that You are as tangible and real to me as I am to myself. I want to walk in Your presence minute by minute. I want to be willing to pray for the people You have placed on my heart. I want to serve You with all my heart, soul, and mind. This all scares me because I know there's a price *to pay. But I still want it. Nothing is worth having unless it is expensive.*

After being totally secure in a relationship with You, I want to meet my husband. I want him to be many things, God. I'm not giving up my broken dreams; I'm just giving them to You so You can put them back together again. I need You to supernaturally give them back to me. I want my husband to serve You 100 percent, with all his heart, soul, and mind. I want him to be dedicated to You at a level that will never be lost or shaken. I want him to be strong yet sensitive. I want him to love me so much (and Nicholas, too, of course) that he would lay down his life for us.

At this point in my writing, I paused. As I finished writing those last words, I saw a vision that impacted me tremendously. I saw Jesus hanging on the cross, His face looking toward the ground. He slowly raised His head and looked into my eyes. Tears streamed down His face, and with a concerned look, He said, "I *did* lay down My life for you."

In that moment, I repented. Jesus' crucifixion took on a whole new meaning in my heart. I needed to stop fantasizing about some mysterious, romantic lover who was going to sweep me off my feet and carry me to paradise. I already *had* a Savior who gave His life for me. My box was opening and my mind expanding. I started to feel God's love pour over me.

On my way to work a few days later, the Garth Brooks song "To Make You Feel My Love" came on the radio. I had to pull to the side of the road because I couldn't see through all my tears. I'm sure I had heard the song before, but now I was hearing it with new ears. Ears that could begin to hear what God was saying to me.

Yes, it's true that Garth was singing the song, but in my car that day, I could swear the Lover of my soul was serenading my heart.

How many times have you dreamed that some guy would write a romantic song just for you? Well, that day the Lord sang to me. I was beginning to see the Lord as the Romancer of my heart. The air was thick with love, the kind of love a teenage girl feels when the quarterback of the football team gives her his letter jacket and he wears her class ring on a chain around his neck. The kind of love every woman longs for when she's watching a romantic movie and envisions herself as the main character.

That week at church, the service was unusually anointed. The lights were dim and I stood in God's presence.

I was immersed in the moment, captivated by His passion for me. I felt Jesus put His arms around me and dance with me. I felt a warm sensation flowing through my spirit and body. I was leaning on the chest of the most perfect Being. I could feel the strength of His neck and I nuzzled my face into that space that felt custom made just for me. I felt so secure, so safe. I could have stayed there all night, just me and Jesus.

When I got home that evening, I opened my Bible to Psalm 139 and read:

> O Lord, you have examined my heart and know everything about me. You know when I sit down or stand up. You know my every thought when far away. You chart the path ahead of me and tell me where to stop and rest. Every moment you know where I am. You know what I am going to say even before I say it, Lord. You both precede and follow me. You place your hand of blessing on my head.

Such knowledge is too wonderful for me, too great for me to know! I can never escape from your spirit! I can never get away from your presence! If I go up to heaven, you are there; if I go down to the place of the dead, you are there. If I ride the wings of the morning, if I dwell by the farthest oceans, even there your hand will guide me, and your strength will support me.

I could ask the darkness to hide me and the light around me to become night—but even in darkness I cannot hide from you. To you the night shines as bright as day. Darkness and light are both alike to you.

You made all the delicate, inner parts of my body and knit me together in my mother's womb. Thank you for making me so wonderfully complex! Your workmanship is marvelous—and how well I know it. You watched me as I was being formed in utter seclusion, as I was woven together in the dark of the womb. You saw me before I was born. Every day of my life was recorded in your book. Every moment was laid out before a single day had passed.

How precious are your thoughts about me, O God! They are innumerable! I can't even count them; they outnumber the grains of sand! And when I wake up in the morning, you are still with me!

O God, if only you would destroy the wicked! Get out of my life, you murderers! They blaspheme you; your enemies take your name in vain. O Lord, shouldn't I hate those who hate you? Shouldn't I despise those who resist you? Yes, I hate them with complete hatred, for your enemies are my enemies.

Search me, O God, and know my heart; test me and know my thoughts. Point out anything in me that offends you, and lead me along the path of everlasting life.[1]

That evening I didn't just write an entry in my journal. I wrote a love letter to the One I was consecrated to, my Beloved.

Jesus,

> *You've done so much for me! You have made it impossible for me to pay You back. I feel such a loyalty to You, not just as a servant or a child, but as a wife! I feel consecrated to You. I want to warn others never to speak against You in any way, for You are my God! You are the One who died to save my life. You died with no guarantee that I would love You in return. That, to me, is the ultimate sacrifice.*

> *You are so wondrous to me! You picked me up when I was beaten down. Words cannot describe the amount of gratitude I feel in my heart for You now, Jesus. You are the Cover of my soul.*

> *Yours forever,*

> *Nicole*

CREATED FOR PARTNERSHIP

I opened my heart up to God, allowing Him to touch the place in my heart reserved just for Him. I felt my priorities fall into order. In the past, I had tried to fill my longing for God with the love of a man. I desired a husband, not realizing that there was an empty space in my life meant for God.

As I meditated on the love of God, a new revelation came to me concerning marriage. The Holy Spirit opened my eyes to see new truths and my heart was transformed.

I realized that God never intended to meet *all* my needs. Now, before you freak out, let me explain! Take a look at Adam. Adam had it made. He had a perfect relationship with God, walking and communing with Him at the deepest level of intimacy. And yet, even in that blessed state, God said, "It is not good for the man to be alone."[2] Adam needed someone to partner with him, so God made provision for him, removing one of his ribs and creating Eve.

When God removed Adam's rib, Adam became incomplete. Eve had something of Adam's, and Adam was incomplete without her. Marriage provided a way for Adam to be whole again.

Under the marriage covenant, man and woman are made "one flesh," emotionally and sexually. God established us on this earth with a need for each other. It is natural to feel this need in your singleness. The drive for intimacy and connection is God given, but we have to remember that God intended it to emerge from perfect communion with Him.

Until this time, I had believed that marriage was a special privilege granted to Christians who had earned it. God revealed to me that, just as He created me for fellowship and communion with Him, He had created me for marriage.

As a single mother, give yourself permission to desire marriage and to desire a father for your child. He absolutely approves of those desires. Just remember that He wants you to experience intimacy and communion with Him as well. In the same way a single mother feels incomplete without a husband, and a child feels incomplete without a father, we are all incomplete without a deep relationship with God.

I've heard many single moms express a secret fear that for some reason, it's not in the cards for them to get married. This is especially true for those who feel they've been waiting a long time. Here are a few things to consider in your season of waiting.

1. You've been praying for your godly prince to come and love you and your child. But that prince may still be a frog, and God may be diligently working on transform-

ing him before sending him your way. Somebody told me once that when you stop looking for your husband, that's when God sends him. So I proceeded to go about life pretending I wasn't looking. I think God probably got a good laugh out of that. I look back now and laugh at myself, so He must've really snickered at my silly games.

2. My pastor once told me, "You attract who you are now, not who you someday hope to be."[5] You want your mate to be mature emotionally, mentally, and spiritually, but you have to become all those things, too, for it to be an equal match. Focus on *becoming* a wonderful mate—a princess worthy of a prince. Think of yourself as a gift to the man you will marry and know that you are responsible for becoming that gift.

When I embraced God's heart for me and understood that He had created me to desire marriage, something within me changed. I felt things break off of me and I no longer felt unnecessary pressure. I was able to relax as a new level of trust invaded my soul.

Dare to dream about the awesome future God is preparing for you. "'For I know the plans I have for you,' says the Lord. 'They are plans for good and not for disaster, to give you a future and a hope.'"[4]

ENDNOTES

1. Psalm 139 (NLT).
2. Genesis 2:18 (NIV).
3. Pastor Danny Silk is the family pastor at Bethel Church in Redding, California. His materials on the issue of family living are available for order at www.ibethel.org.
4. Jeremiah 29:11 (NLT).

CHAPTER 9

Old Friends, New Trials

W hile my transformation in Tennessee was taking place, my best friend, Kim, was on a spiritual journey of her own. Kim had gone to Baylor and experienced personal revival. After she rededicated her life to the Lord, He began to romance her heart much like He did mine.

We kept in touch, maintaining a close friendship despite being separated for many months. She had even been able to visit me in Tennessee and spend some time with her "nephew," Nicholas.

After a semester at Baylor, as much as she enjoyed it there, she became homesick. She decided that her goal had been accomplished in establishing herself in relationship with God again, so she started looking into transferring to Bethel College in Minneapolis, Minnesota. Kim's brother, Jon, lived there, and their home was only seven hours west of the Twin Cities.

In January of our second year apart, I made plans to visit Kim in Minneapolis. Barb volunteered to care for Nicholas; it would be my first vacation since he was born. I was excited to have a weekend of rest and fellowship with my best friend. We had both changed so much. Our relationship had grown deeper and our connection stronger.

When I arrived, Kim and I embraced. It was so good to see her again. She had planned out our weekend with a full schedule of fun activities. She suggested we meet up with her brother and his friends for a night on the town.

I felt a bit apprehensive about that idea. I had spent many days at Kim and Jon's house while growing up, and he and I were well acquainted with each other. We had kind of a love-hate relationship going on. In junior high, it was love. We "dated" for a month and I was his first kiss. But in high school and college, he didn't agree with the way I was living my life and felt I was a bad influence on his sister. He made his disapproval known to me and said some things that really hurt me. After I moved to Tennessee I imagined his opinion of me sank lower upon finding out I was pregnant outside of marriage. Jon was no saint, but his weaknesses were different from mine. He didn't really understand my situation, and I didn't figure he'd have much compassion for what I was going through.

When Kim and I met up with Jon, I was pleasantly surprised and relieved at his openness and his interest in my life. He commented several times about how good I looked, both outwardly and inwardly. He noted that God had made some serious changes in me since we had last been together. He was all smiles and I could tell he was no longer judging me, but sincerely admired the transformation that had taken place in my life. He told me of his recent commitment to quit drinking; he felt it was the only thing holding him back from being "100 percent sold out" to God.

We had a great visit and found that we had more in common than we ever had before. It was the beginning of treasured friendship.

THE FLIGHT HOME

Almost as soon as my trip began, it seemed to be over. I had missed Nicholas terribly, but it was still difficult to say good-bye to Kim. After that visit, I asked God to make a way for us to be near each other more often.

During my flight home, I had some time to reflect on the previous two years of my life. God had plucked me from everything that was familiar to me and sent me on a truly incredible journey. I had walked through intense healing and deliverance from my past, experienced deep wounds and rejection from Michael, and was picked up, dusted off, and set on course again. God had given me vision for my destiny and planted amazing gifts within me that were beginning to manifest themselves in my life and ministry. He had surrounded me with faithful, dedicated friends and mentors, many of whom loved my son and me. God was bringing me each month into new levels of trust and faith, and He had given me peace about my current circumstances. I had arrived at a High Place, a spiritual mountain, and it felt great!

January 2

Well, Jesus, it's a new year, and I have so much to discuss with You. I'm thankful to have the relationship with You that I do. I'm glad You are so mighty and that Your ways are not my ways. I know that You have plans for me and that they are good plans, plans to add to my life and bring me joy. Not joy from this world, but perfect joy that can only come from You. God, I could spend all day writing about what You have done for me. I could write a seven-series book on that alone!

Even though it's hard, I still want to give everything to You. I want my life to be a pure reflection of Your love. I want everything about me to honor You. I'm such a passionate person, so motivated. I want to make sure I give it all back to You.

I wanted more of God. In His goodness, He continued to answer my prayers, but in unexpected ways.

Dear Jesus,

Tonight I feel a bit confused. Sometimes I'm supposed to come to You with childlike faith, and other times I'm supposed to know how to do all these complicated things. I want to take this one step at a time. I really don't want a career. I don't want to spend forty hours a week at work. I'd rather be doing other things, like spending time with Nicholas, meditating on Your Word, and working in ministry. I know I told You, "Not my will, but Yours be done," and I meant it. I'm just having a hard time right now. I feel weary. I would like a break from it all. I would like to pass the baton off for a little while. However, I know that in the end, it is not what You can do for me, but more what I can do for You.

So what can I do, Lord, that will bring about honor? Point it out to me and I will work toward it. Perfect that which is imperfect, Lord. Put me through the fire, but PLEASE go with me. I need Your strength to endure it all, Lord. Sometimes it gets a little overwhelming. I feel like I'm lacking something, but I don't know exactly what it is. Please reveal to me in the next moments of my life where my next turn is. Don't let my enemies overcome me. For "thou, O Lord, art a shield for me; my glory, and the lifter up of mine head."[1]

I love You!

NEW LEVELS OF FAITH

About a week after that journal entry, Nicholas came down with the flu. The day-care center called me that afternoon and insisted I pick him up and take him home. His flu continued for a few days. Unable to take him to day care, I had to stay home from work to care for him. Finally my boss called. I had kind of expected to hear what he had to say, but the words still stung my heart. "This isn't working out for us. We're going to have to let you go."

God had been so faithful to me, yet I still cringed when it happened. I began to panic. I had never had to walk in this much faith!

That afternoon, I frantically wrote e-mails to people, making a plea to "pray, pray, pray." I needed God to provide another job, and *soon*!

I filled out every job application available to me. I had no credit cards and no savings account, no financial cushion to support me. Days turned into weeks, and I found myself in a serious dilemma.

One day, as I was reading the Word and spending time with the Lord, I heard Him say, "Remember all those people who said to you, at one time or another, 'If you ever need anything, ask'?"

I said, "Yes, Lord. I remember a few people."

He replied, "Well, it's time to ask."

Now, it was one thing to constantly plead with the Lord for money; it was quite another to swallow my pride and ask my friends and family. But at this point, my back was against the wall and I had no other options. Until then, I had never directly asked anyone for financial support.

I started with my pastor, my friend Kim, her brother Jon, and a few relatives. I couldn't bring myself to ask on the phone or in person, so I wrote everyone letters.

As I waited to receive answers, I pounded the pavement, looking high and low for a job. One man almost hired me. He was very sympathetic to my situation. But since I lacked a few qualifications, he decided to hire someone else. He ended our conversation, "If you ever need anything, please ask. I will try to make it happen." When he made that offer, I wanted to cry out, "I need lots of help!" I couldn't do it, though, so he got a note in the mail as well.

THE WIDOW'S MITE

During this season, I lived every day in a state of anxiety. I tried hard not to worry about my provision, but ten weeks passed with no hope of getting a job.

One day, I was reading a magazine, and one line caught my eye. Someone had once asked Billy Graham who the major contributors to his ministry were. He explained that there were no major contributors; it was the widow's mite that kept the ministry running.

When I read those words, I heard the Lord say, "You have twenty dollars left in your wallet. That is your mite, all you have left in the world. I want you to give that money to this ministry."

This was one of those times when I desperately wanted to pretend I had not heard God's voice clearly. I thought, *You've got to be kidding me, God!* But He was not kidding, and I knew He wasn't. I thought, *This is going to be the greatest sacrifice I've ever made.*

I don't remember how much food I had left in the pantry, but I do know that I was behind a couple of months on the rent and my car payment was overdue. In fact, there were days when I fully expected someone to come and repossess my vehicle. So, painful as it was, I got out a pen and some paper and wrote a letter to this ministry explaining why I was giving them my last twenty dollars.

Almost as soon as I sent it off in the mail, things began to turn around. As I look back, I see that my level of sacrifice brought an equal level of breakthrough.

BREAKTHROUGH

That evening, someone at church gave me twenty dollars. I thought, *That's pretty cool.* Every day the next week, I went to the mailbox and found envelopes full of checks—$300, $200, $50, $100. Everyone to whom I had written answered and reached out to me with love *and money*!

There were still no job interviews, but one day, the man who almost hired me rang my doorbell. Embarrassed, I didn't want to open the door. But I also didn't want to miss out on a much-needed blessing, so I overcame my shame and opened the door. He stood there with his wallet open. "How much do you need?" he asked. I couldn't bring myself to say a dollar amount, so I shared that I had been out of work for quite a while and bills were piling up. He reached in his wallet, handed me $300 in cash, and then walked away, wishing blessings upon my son and me!

My heart was beginning to beat normally again as I reached a new level of trust in the Lord. Even when I didn't do a thing to earn it, He was able to supernaturally provide for my needs. Although I was out of work for sixteen weeks, I did not get evicted, I did not lose my car, and Nicholas and I were eating!

That last week of unemployment, I went to my mailbox and nearly collapsed when I read the letter that was waiting for me.

It was from the ministry into which I had sown my last twenty dollars. The evangelist had read my letter and was so moved by my obedience that he decided to send me $150 in return! God was truly blessing my socks off.

Despite the breakthrough and the blessing, this was a season of great difficulty. There were days of great sorrow intermingled with moments of relief. Generally, I felt really lost. I couldn't understand the season I was in and I longed for God to show me when it would all end.

Dear Jesus,

I want to record some Scriptures that You have given me to get through this trying season.

Luke 11:9–10. So I say to you, ask, and it will be given to you; seek, and you will find; knock, and it will be opened to you. For everyone who asks receives, and he who seeks finds, and to him who knocks it will be opened.

John 14:27, 29. Peace I leave with you, My peace I give to you; not as the world gives do I give to you. Let not your heart be troubled, neither let it be afraid. . . . And now I have told you before it comes, that when it does come to pass, you may believe.

1 Peter 4:12–13 (NLT). Dear friends, don't be surprised at the fiery trials you are going through, as if something strange were happening to you. Instead, be very glad—because these trials will make you partners with Christ in his suffering.

Isaiah 50:7–9. For the Lord God will help Me; therefore I will not be disgraced; therefore I have set My face like a flint, and I know that I will not be ashamed.

Isaiah 51:12, 16 (NCT). I, even I, am the one who comforts you. . . . And I have put my words in your mouth and hidden you safely within my hand.

Isaiah 60:22 (NIV). I am the Lord; in its time I will do this swiftly.

Yesterday as I was searching for a job and waiting to hear a response, I broke down. I basically threw a fit and questioned You and Your will for my life. I demanded certain things from You, and that was so wrong. After I talked to Dad, I realized how wrong I was. I was murmuring and complaining just like the Israelites, Lord.

I repent from the bottom of my heart. I am ashamed of my words, my mind-set, and my demands. Please forgive me, Father. I should know by now that You truly do have my life in Your hands. The Word says that You hold the waters of the earth in the palm of Your hand. Surely You can handle my problems!

Forgive me for my doubt, my unbelief, and my complaining. I truly do want to replace all those words with praise. Through this crushing, remold me into what You desire. I do not wish to be crushed like this again. Teach me the lessons so I won't have to stay in the fire any longer. I believe Your promise that when this is all through, I will be as gold, pure and refined. You will be able to hold me for the world to see.

Thank You for my life. Thank You for the good plans You have for me. Last night at church, You had someone come up to me and say that everything truly is going to work out. You are taking care of my situation and are willing to handle it. I receive that word, Lord. No more worry strengthens my bond with Nicholas and helps me to be a good mother. Let us be as close as a mother and son can be.

Thank You again, Father, for sticking with me through all this. You are truly faithful always, even when I'm not. I love You, Lord, today and forever. You are my God, the Rock on which I stand.

ATLANTA

In the midst of this trial, Jon e-mailed me to tell me he was traveling to Atlanta for a friend's wedding. He wanted to know if I'd like to drive down to visit while he was in the area. Barb took care of Nicholas for me. For one weekend I was able to lay down my concerns and hang out with a dear friend. By this time, our friendship had really grown and I considered Jon to be my personal "Jonathan." In the Bible Jonathan had been a covenantal friend of David's, one who stuck closer than a brother.

We stayed at Jon's friend's house and I got to meet a group of his friends from college. It was a relaxing weekend. The night before I left we stayed up late visiting. I ended up falling asleep with my head in his lap. The next day, we said our good-byes, and as I got in my car to drive home, I found money that he had secretly stashed for me to buy gas. My heart warmed at the gesture and I felt extremely glad that I had spent the weekend with him.

Though this all sounds extremely romantic, at the time, he was only a much-needed friend, and I deliberately was not "going there" in my mind.

That week, Jon sent me pictures of us at the wedding along with a note that hinted he had "gone there." I smiled, but felt a bit scared at the same time.

NORTH DAKOTA

I was beginning to feel in my spirit that my time in Tennessee was coming to an end. I was so tired and weary that I wanted only to fall into the arms of my family. I searched the Lord earnestly for an answer and I laid out a fleece before Him to make sure I was in His will.[2] If I was to stay in Tennessee, I asked Him to provide a job for me by the end of the month.

Well, the end of the month came, and I was jobless. I believed that was a way of God confirming what I had already felt in my heart. I began selling everything. All Nicholas and I kept were our clothes and whatever else I could fit in my little Eagle Talon. I asked my grandma and grandpa if they would be willing to open their doors to Nicholas and me. They assured me we were welcome. As I made plans, I wrestled with doubt.

After a Sunday night service, a stranger approached me and prayed over me. She said, "God told me that He is going to restore to you the joy of your salvation and that what you're planning to do right now is His will. He said to tell you that you are walking exactly in the steps that He would have you walk." After that night, my doubts were gone and I felt confident in my decision to move home. I felt blessed that God was still with me, guiding my every step.

It was difficult to say good-bye to my dear friends in Tennessee. Barb and her family tried to talk me out of my decision, but I knew it was time to go. We all cried many tears together. I knew I would always have affection for Tennessee, and for my friends, mentors, and spiritual family who helped me through the fire.

Once everything was packed, I took Nicholas to spend one more night with Barb while I rested up for the drive. At five a.m., I picked up my baby from her house and began our trip home. As I drove away, I wondered what God had in store for Nicholas and me.

ENDNOTES

1. Psalm 3:3 (KJV).
2. See Judges 6: 36–40. To "put out a fleece" before the Lord is to ask Him for a specific confirmation before we take action. Gideon received a promise that God would save Israel through his hand. The night before he went to battle, Gideon laid out a piece of lamb's wool (referred to as a fleece) and asked the Lord for a sign: If the fleece was damp and the ground was dry, he would take it as a sign or confirmation that God would do as He promised. In times of great need, we can ask God for confirmation in such a way. However, I would like to stress that God's answers to these "fleeces" we put out will *never* contradict His Word. If we receive such a contradictory response, we are misinterpreting His reply, probably due to our own desires. In addition, we should always look for other confirmations to back up the "fleece." If something truly is His will, He will make it known to you if you ask in openness and sincerity.

CHAPTER 10

Returning Home

God was with me as I drove the twenty-three hours to North Dakota, where another aunt and uncle lived. It was three a.m. when my little car finally stopped in their driveway. I stumbled up to the house with my sleeping baby to crash for the night. I felt blessed to be with family again, and I took a full day to rest and visit before the last leg of our trip.

When I finally made it to my grandparents' house, my grandma came out to greet me with hugs and smiles. I rested in her arms, knowing that for a while, someone was going to take care of us.

Over the next month, I soaked it all in—the farm, the horses, my family, the freedom. I began to go to church with Grandma and Grandpa. At one of the first services there, I saw Kim and Jon's mom and dad (Ruby and Gerald). They hadn't seen me since before I was pregnant. I was a different person now.

Ruby's face glowed when she saw me, and she hugged me tightly. They were all glad to have Nicholas and me home at last. Ruby taught Nicholas in Sunday school and immediately bonded with him. She often bought us diapers and invited us to Happy Valley Ranch, their farm just a few miles down the road from where we lived.

I often talked to Kim about finding a place where we could live together. All these years of friendship, but we had never been roommates. One day I told her, "What would be really awesome is if Jon would buy a house, and we could all live together."

She smiled and said, "Yes, what about Jon?"

"What about him? He's like my brother!"

"But what if he were something else?"

I quickly changed the subject. It was not the first time someone had tried to set me up with their brother or son. I didn't know who God was going to send, but I was certain it was not going to be someone I had known my whole life. I had a hunch my future husband was going to be some stranger from a far-off land—a foreign prince or something.

I had thought long and hard about what I wanted in a husband. Here were some of the expectations I jotted down:

1. I want a mate who loves the Lord God with all his heart, soul, and mind.

2. I want a mate who is Spirit filled and led daily by the Holy Spirit.

3. I want a mate who is sensitive to the Lord and teachable.

4. I want a mate who is as Christlike as possible.

5. I want him to consider me a good wife and helpmate, and when he finds me, to pursue me until he wins my heart.

6. I want him to be open and honest always, willing to communicate and be productive.

7. I want him to have a supernatural affection and love for Nicholas, willing to raise him, love him, and accept him as his own, and to be an example of Christ to him.

8. I want him to have a vision and a goal for life. I want him to have passion and ambition about everything he does.

9. I want him to love me as Christ loves the church.

10. I want to have an intimacy with him that surpasses any other relationship, save my relationship with Christ.

11. I want him to be my greatest advocate, and I desire to be his.

12. I want him to take the role of being the priest of his home, covering his family daily in prayer.

13. I want him to be capable of providing well for us.

14. I want to be physically attracted to him and I pray he would be very affectionate with me always.

15. I want him to be a leader, and I want him to be strong as well as wise.

16. I want him to have a good sense of family, the way God intended.

17. I want the faith of Joshua to be in him; I want the love and sensitivity of David to fall on him; I want the dedication and loyalty of Paul to saturate him; I want the mighty man of valor to rise up in him as it did in Gideon; I want the leadership abilities of Moses to guide him.

18. I pray he would have a soft heart and he would walk in love.

19. I pray he would prosper in all he does, and that he have a generous, giving heart.

20. I pray the anointing of God would rest heavily on his life.

I thanked God for this wonderful husband I knew He was preparing for me!

October 7

Dear Jesus, I am torn. I'm not sure what I should be praying right now. You know the things I need even before I ask, so it feels silly to spend my time asking for a bunch of stuff right now. But I want to talk to You about "stuff." Is that okay?

I feel like I've been given a fresh start. I've wanted to listen to all my tapes, read books, and study Your Word. I've been dreaming of my ministry again. I'm hopeful and excited about my future and I feel like my spirit has been stirred and I've received a second wind. I see myself using my gifts and growing in You tremendously this year. I feel more dependent on You and it's a good feeling.

Right now, my future is uncertain, seemingly undetermined. Yet it always amazes me how pliable I become during these seasons of the "unknown." I guess that's why You have me in this season, right?

One thing that makes me happy is that, through it all, I've learned to trust in Jesus, and I have not grown bitter. I do get frustrated at times, but for the most part, I feel like I've kept my heart open to You. Lord, still desiring to serve You with my whole life.

It's good to know that none of this is a result of my own efforts—it's all been by Your grace. I'm glad because You and I both know that if it had been up to me, I would've messed things up.

I thank You in advance for meeting all of my needs. You are awesome!

TRANSITION AND FAVOR

Because the spiritual culture at home was so drastically different from Tennessee, I began to search out more of God's presence. One afternoon, my mom called me to tell me about a prophetic minister who was coming to a little church in a neighboring town. I still felt a bit lost, unsure of what my future held. Every category of my life seemed to end in a question mark—work? husband? home?

As I was driving to the church, I felt assured that God would meet me there. I can't explain it entirely with words, but I *knew,* in the pit of my stomach, that the prophet would have a word for me.

My mom and I sat together and the service was great. The speaker's name was Tom, and my heart leaped as he preached. My spiritual hunger was being satisfied. As he concluded the service, he pointed to me and asked me to stand. He said:

> As you walked in the building this evening, the Lord began to tell me things about you. He wanted me to tell you that He has big things in store for you. He has been watching you and He has been arranging things for you. He is going to bless you with a new job, and He wants me to remind you, when you are coming and going and surrounded by blessings, not to forget that it was His hand and His blessings that got you there.

Not long after that I saw the message come to pass. A new company started up not far from where I lived. I scheduled an interview and was hired. The pay was better than I had ever received. During the training process, I was singled out with five others to be promoted to manager. I was flabbergasted. Never in my life had I made this kind of money! And more than that, I loved my job! It seemed too good to be true. I was finally experiencing the second level of provision that I had learned from studying Ruth. I was no longer gleaning for just enough (and sometimes not enough). Now I received enough for myself and some for others around me. I gave full glory to the Lord, just like Tom had reminded me to. I knew He had done this for me.

Dear Jesus,

Well, You have certainly blessed me with this job, Lord. It is one of the greatest opportunities I have ever had. It's been two years, God. That's just a blink of Your eye, but I felt I would never get there. And if I understood You correctly, and if my life really is like Ruth's, then I should soon meet my Boaz! Sometimes I have a peace about it, and sometimes I don't. Sometimes I feel myself getting envious over other people's marriages and engagements. When I hear married people complain, I want to shake them and say, "Don't you know what you have?" I guess it's true that you don't know what you've got till it's gone.

I pray, Lord, that You would keep me during this time. Help me to feel content no matter what situation I face. Please give me the same grace that Paul received to get through the trials he faced. Give me the joy that Paul had, the joy that sustained him through prison and torture. Help me to take advantage of what I have with You now as a single person.

As Your bride, I would officially like to make a date with you this weekend, Jesus.

WHERE IS MY BOAZ?

Once again, I found myself divided. On one hand I was completely content. I had supportive family surrounding me, an amazing job that fulfilled me and paid me extremely well, and a wonderfully sweet son who continually brought me joy. In all these areas of my life, my cup was running over. When I focused on all the Lord had given me, I was overwhelmed with joy. But there were days when my focus shifted to the one thing that still had not come: a husband. There weren't even any hopeful prospects.

Restlessness rose up within me, and at times I simply could not contain it, no matter what I did. And so, I wrestled with God.

Dear Jesus,

Tonight has been a hard night. I have been thinking so much about my husband. Lord, I wish You would send him. I am so lonely. I don't know how much longer I can bear being alone. Almost everyone around me has found a mate. It's getting so hard for me, knowing that Nicholas is growing up without a father. I feel so frustrated. I wish You would either give me some answers or send him. I mean it, Lord. I need You to communicate with me. I need You to let me know what You're doing with my life.

You know my heart, Lord. You know that no matter how hard it gets, and no matter how many times I mess up, I will stay faithful and loyal to You. All I ask, Lord, as You ask of me, is that in this relationship You would communicate with me.

I also know that You communicate with us in several different ways, and I've come to recognize Your voice in many areas, whether it be in a song, a Scripture, a book, a word of knowledge, or a dream. Lord, You've used all those ways before, so I'm asking You to do it again.

I'm really desperate, Lord. Every time I've come to this place before, You've met me. So I believe You will again. I believe You've studied me and You've watched me since I was born. You've been there at every turn of my life.

Why can't I grow in You with a husband at my side, Lord? You designed it to be that way, so how can I be wrong to ask? Especially when You consider Nicholas and his needs.

I feel empty right now. I've been seeking You night after night, but I don't feel You responding like I used to. I know Your Spirit is here, Father, just like it was in Tennessee. I know You can meet me here and Your presence can fall on me just as it did there. So why doesn't it? Why are You so quiet? I know You're not distant. So will You answer me? Will You guide me? I want to know You're here. I want to feel Your presence. I feel like You're holding Yourself at arm's length. I feel like You're keeping me isolated. Why, God? You know what it is I'm craving, Father: intimacy and companionship.

I'm sorry for my impatience. I do feel Your peace, Lord. Sometimes I feel such an urge to get married it almost consumes me. Lord Jesus, it awakens a deeper hunger in me to experience Your glory. I desire Your presence, Your power. I desire You, Lord.

Lord, I am in one of those situations tonight where I really don't care what I hear from You, I just need to hear something. I've experienced so many drastic changes in the past three years, and I don't know what to think of most of it. I must've gone through all of this for a reason.

Remember when I felt You telling me my Boaz was coming? Well, I don't feel like any of that has happened yet. I wish I knew without a doubt that those words were from You.

The Bible says it perfectly when it says, "Hope deferred makes the heart sick." (Proverbs 13:12 NLT) Then it adds, "But when dreams come true, there is life and joy." Maybe I can hang on to those words a little longer, if You give me the strength, Lord.

WHAT ABOUT JON?

One night I heard a still small voice say, *What about Jon?* Others had asked me that same question—Kim, Mom, my friends—and I never hesitated to say, "I don't think we have a romantic future." But in that moment, I looked at his picture on my bed stand and I asked myself, "What *about* Jon?"

I grabbed my journal and flipped to the entry where I had written about my future mate. I furiously read it through, and with each line, I could feel something happening in my heart. I had a revelation: Jon fulfilled every one of these (or at least he was well on his way).

Then a weird thing happened to me. I don't know if I can describe it accurately in words. Suddenly, I felt a love for Jon that I had never felt before. The timing was perfect. It was as if God had been hiding my own feelings from me and, all of a sudden, He snatched the curtain away and there they were! I thought, *This could be the real thing.*

That night I tossed and turned, thinking about what all this could mean. I reflected over the past year, thinking about how often we had e-mailed each other and how quickly our friendship had grown. I thought about how close Nicholas already was to Kim and Ruby. Everything made sense. It makes sense to marry your best friend!

After taking a few days to think about this new development, I broke down and called Kim. I asked her what she thought of this "craziness." She was very excited and didn't think it odd at all. I could tell by her response that anything Jon had said about me was very positive, although she didn't share details. I asked her not to tell Jon about any of my newfound feelings because I was still working through all of it, trying to figure out if it was real. The last thing I wanted was for Jon to be hurt. I told her I was going to pray about it before saying anything.

As I prayed, I asked the Lord for another confirmation. I knew Jon was coming home to the ranch for Christmas, and I knew I'd be spending time there with him and his family. I asked the Lord to make my feelings stronger for him during this time if I was to consider him something more than a good friend. I decided it was a good test.

In the meantime, I focused on my daily life, achieving excellence at my job, as a mom, and in my relationship with the Lord. Jon was in my thoughts often, but I still had several weeks before I could put my feelings to the test. Time flew by awfully fast, and before long, Christmas was right around the corner.

CHAPTER 11

Christmas

It was a crisp, glistening white morning in North Dakota. Kim was coming home from Minneapolis with Jon, and I was filled with anticipation. Ruby had invited Nicholas and me to Happy Valley Ranch to spend the day with their family, and I accepted. It was going to be a day of family, friends, food, and games. I couldn't wait. By the time we were dressed and ready to go, it was almost noon on Christmas Day.

We rushed into Ruby's front entry to escape the cold winter wind, and we were instantly warmed with smiles and hugs. It was so good to see my best friend, Kim. Nicholas took no time to make himself at home, finding adventure in exploring Ruby's kitchen cabinets. Jon was outside helping his dad with chores, so we didn't get to connect right away. Kim and I went to her bedroom, plopped ourselves down on her bed, and caught up on all that was new with each other. She told me about nursing school and her upcoming trip to Israel. I told her all about my new job and the satisfaction of actually having some money to spend.

After we spent some time together, Kim bundled up Nicholas and took him outside to play in the snow. I went upstairs to join in on the games that were going on.

When Jon came in a little later, my heart skipped a beat as he headed my way. He greeted me warmly and proceeded to rub my shoulders as if it were the most natural thing to do. The whole day seemed to be filled with smiles and hugs. After just a few hours, I felt my heart swelling with affection for this man.

Nicholas came in and started running around, yelling, "Don! Don! Don!" (He couldn't say "Jon" yet.) Jon brought out his old farm toys, Matchbox cars, and GI Joes so Nicholas could play with them. It was all so much to absorb. Sometimes I wonder how I made it through that Christmas without exploding with joy. The whole day, I wanted to do cartwheels right there in the living room.

To end the night, Kim, Jon, Nicholas, and I went downstairs to watch a movie. I desperately wanted to lay on Jon's chest and snuggle up with him. I knew it wasn't the right time, but I did inch as close to him as possible without being *too* obvious. When the movie was over, we all said our good-byes and hugged, and Nicholas and I drove back to Grandma and Grandpa's house.

NO LONGER A MYSTERY

After spending Christmas with Jon and his family, I was no longer wondering about my feelings for him. My attraction to him was increasing, and I knew God had answered my prayer. But I hadn't thought about the next step. I had asked for guidance from the Lord and He had answered me, but now what? What should I say? "It's great that you're home for Christmas. Oh, and by the way, I'm in love with you!"

I was beginning to feel the way Ruth must have felt as she waited at Boaz's feet. I knew God was calling me to the "threshing floor" with Jon. He was asking me to make myself vulnerable before him. But in my heart I wondered, *Do I have Ruth's courage?*

We spent the next day much like the day before, filling ourselves with family, food, and fellowship. That night Nicholas debuted in his first Christmas play. He was two years old and excited to be on stage. Since Ruby was his Sunday school teacher, she had taught him the song "Away in a Manger" with all the hand movements.

Both Kim's family and mine went to see Nicholas perform. The little Baptist church was packed. I squeezed into the pew with Kim and Jon on either side of me. As the play started, I realized that I didn't have to watch my son's first play by myself. I sat next to the man I loved, and he watched Nicholas with eyes full of affection. I hoped nobody noticed the tears in my eyes, and if they did notice, I hoped they would think I was just an emotional mother. I was, of course. But I was also a little overwhelmed by the volts of electricity that kept shooting through my body every time I felt Jon tightening his arm around my shoulder.

When the play ended, our families went our separate ways. That was a good thing because my head was reeling with all the excitement. I felt like a giddy teenager and couldn't stop smiling.

Right in front of the rest of my family, my aunt asked, "Who was that good-lookin' man who had his arm around you at church tonight?"

I felt my face flush, so I decided to bear my heart. "Okay, everyone," I said, "if you would pick anyone for me to marry, who would it be?"

A shout arose in unison: "Jon!"

THE LETTER

As I went to bed that night, I thought about the fact that the next day would be Jon's last day in town. After church he would jump into his car and return to Minneapolis. I was running out of time to make my feelings known to him.

When the next morning did arrive, Jon didn't sit with me during the church service. I felt a little confused. I didn't know what to make of it. I wondered if he was drawing back from me.

After the service, I expected some kind of grand good-bye. (It has to be dramatic, doesn't it?) Instead, it was just a simple "bye" and he was off.

I went back to work on December 27, still struggling to make sense of it all. I couldn't talk to Kim because she was on the road, traveling back to Minnesota. I asked the Lord for a game plan.

By the next day, I had it. That morning, I awoke with an urgent desire to write to Jon. It seemed risky, but the urgency would not subside. I wrote the most intense e-mail of my life.

Dear Jon,

This is going to be the most difficult e-mail I have ever typed, but I am not going to beat around the bush. I'm just going to tell you what's on my heart. I believe that taking the direct approach is best in this situation. We are both honest, straightforward people. So here goes . . .

My life seems to have taken a turn and I'm not sure what to do about it. I've been praying about this, of course, and thinking a lot about it. In the past few months, I feel like my feelings for you have changed. You have always been a good friend, and especially in the past two years, you've been a friend who "sticks closer than a brother." As I've mentioned before, our friendship could be compared to David and Jonathan. I felt like we have true kindred spirits, something you don't find very often in a lifetime. You have prayed for me and been a source of strength for me during some of the most difficult times of my life. I feel tied to you in my heart, Jon. If not for your support, I don't know how I would've made it through. Is it any wonder that my heart would someday be overwhelmed with feelings for you?

For a long time, I pushed thoughts of you aside because I decided that you were a brother in Christ, a friend sent by God, nothing more. I thought that finding "the one" had to be more complicated. But the time we have spent together over the past year has changed my mind.

This is what I need to know: Would you think of pursuing a relationship with me beyond friendship? I'm sorry I had to e-mail all this, but I chickened out when I tried to tell you face to face!

This is really scary for me, Jon. I don't remember a time when I was this honest and vulnerable. But that's okay because I trust you, and I know that no matter what happens, you would never hurt me. I also know and believe that God is in control. If you don't feel the same way I do, then it isn't meant to be. That's okay too. I trust God that He knows what's best for me. He sees ALL when I can only see what's right in front of me.

I guess before I pray about "us" anymore, or even think about it anymore, I need to know your feelings and thoughts about all this. As long as we can remain totally honest with each other, we will always have our friendship.

I'll be waiting to hear from you. I have so much more to say to you, but until I know how you feel, I can't really go into it all.

I hope you made it home safe. I look forward to hearing from you.

Love,

Nicole

(P.S. Nicholas says he misses you.)

I wrote the letter on Monday morning. Writing it was not the hardest part despite what I had thought. I soon found out I didn't have the courage to click the "Send" button. I paced around the room, trying to talk myself out of it. My thoughts were a blur. I hadn't told anyone that I wanted to share my life with Jon; maybe I should wait and talk to Kim. As I reread the words I had written, I felt more love for him with every sentence. After hours of debating, I asked my grandma to come and push the button for me.

I did not get much sleep that night. I wondered how long I would have to wait to hear back from him. When I woke up the next day, December 29, I rushed to my computer to check my e-mail. Nothing.

During the course of the day, I probably checked my e-mails about once or twice a minute! By five p.m. I had still received no response. I was beginning to get nervous because I knew Jon checked his e-mail every day.

As soon as I got home, I shut myself up in my bedroom and wrote this entry in my journal.

Dear Jesus,

Oh, Lord! Now I've really gone and done it. I've bared my soul to another human being. All I can do now is wait. Lord, I feel like this had to be You. How could these sudden feelings of love pop out of nowhere? I am coming to You tonight vulnerable and scared. I need

Your peace, Lord. Thank You for Psalm 84:11–12: "For the Lord God is a sun and shield; the Lord will give grace and glory; no good thing will he withhold from those who walk uprightly. O Lord of hosts, blessed is the man who trusts in You!"

I also love Philippians 4:6–7: "Be anxious for nothing, but in everything by prayer and supplication, with thanksgiving, let your requests be made known to God; and the peace of God, which surpasses all understanding, will guard your hearts and minds through Christ Jesus."

After going over Your Word, Lord, I interpret my situation like this: I need to rest in Your peace. If what I'm asking for is going to benefit me, Your daughter, You will not hesitate to give it to me. Right? So since my heart has not stopped racing, how do I really receive Your peace? I guess I need to ask for more faith, Lord, more faith to believe all that I wrote with all my heart, soul, and mind.

Before I went to bed, I checked my e-mail once more. And there it was, a response from Jon. I clicked on it. My heart pounded as I read his words.

Dear Nicole,

Thanks for the e-mail. I know how hard it is to write those types of letters. I especially know how hard it was in this case, because I wrote a letter like this to you on the plane ride back from Atlanta this summer. In the end, I decided against sending it because I wanted to wait for something, a sign or a different time—I'm not sure.

Well, now I have the sign, and I have to admit I am scared. I am not scared of the commitment to you and Nicholas. I'm scared about not doing the will of God. What if this is the easy way out for us? What if we are both lonely and are reading into the situation? I don't know. I do know that I need to pray about this, and I need some time to think and seek advice.

If we do decide to go further in our relationship, I don't plan on breaking it off unless it is plainly God's will to do so. I mean, I don't want to be in your life as a friend one minute, more than a friend for a while, and then back to being a friend again. That would be painful for everybody and confusing for Nicholas. Am I making any sense?

What do you think? Can you give me some time to pray?

Love,

Jon

I reread the e-mail several times. His response was not as definitive as I had hoped, but I deeply respected his desire to seek the Lord on the matter before answering me. He really cared about Nicholas and me, and he wasn't going to rush into something this serious without hearing from God and getting counsel from trusted friends.

I replied, trying to take some of the pressure off of him as he ventured out to make his decision.

Jon,

Well, thank God I got your e-mail today. I was about ready to crawl out of my skin. This has been a stressful day, to say the least.

I can completely understand where you're coming from. I have had the same thoughts run over and over in my mind. But let me tell you what made me write to you. I assure you, if I had not been sure about this, I would never have written you.

First let me say that I know it was God who stopped you from sending that letter to me this summer. I wasn't ready then. There are many reasons it wouldn't have worked back then. First of all, it would have made me wonder if I was moving back to North Dakota because of God or because of you. There were many issues I had to deal with before I would've been ready for another relationship. There are also many things that God has done in my life that He might not have been able to do had I been in a relationship with you. And, to be honest, I still thought of you as a brother.

Next, I want to talk about what confirmed for me that this is God's will. Yes, I have been lonely, and yes, I have wanted God to send my husband to me. But I was willing to wait on God. I was not going to risk making the wrong decision by choosing the first good candidate who came along. I knew that by acting too quickly I would not be the only one to suffer. So I made a pact with God that no matter how long it took, I would wait for the man He chose for Nicholas and me. I trusted Him enough to make that decision for us.

About four weeks ago, I realized you were coming home for Christmas. As always, I was looking forward to seeing you. But the feeling was nothing out of the ordinary. Things were busy for me and life was moving along. But one day, it hit me. I thought, Why not Jon? At first, I panicked and thought, I'm just lonely right now, and I'm reaching for him because he's dear to me. But the thought did not leave, and still hasn't.

I prayed and prayed and prayed. I got out one of my journals and turned back to an entry in which I had told God what I desired in a husband and a father for Nicholas. I read each item on the list, and when I was done, I cried. You fit every single requirement. Not most of them, Jon. All of them. This was one of many confirmations I received.

Nicholas weighed heavily on my mind, of course. I am very sensitive in the area of his future father. I've watched you with him since the first time you two met. It has touched my heart the way he's taken to you. When I think about it, I can't imagine anyone else in this world being a better father.

You have been so faithful to me. The fact that you lifted me up in prayer shows me that, if you would do it as a friend, you would do it as a husband. This is so important to me.

There were many other confirmations, Jon. Things people said, things people did. I can understand your state of mind right now, but I'm convinced. I asked for certain things and God came through. He let me know beyond a shadow of a doubt. And I know that if it's truly His will, He will do the same for you.

The fact that you are concerned about Nicholas not getting confused in the process means the world to me. You have a level of integrity and character that most people don't have.

I agree with you 100 percent that this shouldn't be some "trial period" type of relationship. I think we should pray, hear from the Lord, and go with what He says. Basically what you said. If we do it, we do it. No turning back. I realize this is serious. It involves not only our hearts, but the hearts of those around us. So I am going to pray like I never have before.

I want you to take as much time as you need. I encourage you to pray and seek as much godly wisdom as possible. I trust you, Jon. Whatever you decide I will know that you put a lot of effort into it.

Thanks for writing me back.

Love,

Nicole

Dear Jesus,

I feel okay now. I know that Jon's the one. I still trust You, Father. I believe You know what's best for the three of us. I pray for Jon during this time, that he would be able to hear Your voice clearly. I pray his heart would receive all You have to say to him about our future. But most of all, God, I pray You would bear his burdens for him so that he could cast his cares on You and You would carry him through this potentially stressful decision-making season.

Help me to stay focused on You through it all. I pray a protection over both of us that we would not be deceived in any way. I know we both want Your will. We are so ready to comply. We just need a clear answer. We know and trust that You have good plans for our lives.

My first obligation is to You, Lord, and it will always, always be that way. You mean more to me than this life I live. I want so much to please You. I feel so much gratitude toward You, Lord, for who You made me to be. I have been so lost at times, but You never gave up on me. You're the only one who has always loved me unconditionally. You've come through on promises before, and I know You'll come through this time as well. Guard my heart and guard Jon's heart. But most important, show us Your will. Please, Daddy.

CHAPTER 12

A Man's Perspective

When I (Jon) first saw Nicole after Nicholas was born, I was amazed at her transformation. She was as beautiful as ever, but her glowing countenance reflected a deep inward change. She constantly spoke of the Lord and all He was doing in her life. Over the course of her visit to Minneapolis, something began stirring within me. On the last night of her visit, we were hanging out, playing cards with some friends. It was that night that God dropped a bomb on me. In my spirit I heard Him say, "I want you to marry this woman and take care of her."

Nicole returned to Tennessee, and I confided in my sister, Kim, all that had transpired. In her opinion, it was not God who had spoken to me that night, but my own heart. She reminded me that I was lonely and was currently on a quest to find my future wife. Perhaps my heart had merely played a trick on me.

Although I trust my sister's counsel, I could not forget what had happened. Day after day, I poured myself out in prayer for Nicole and Nicholas.

After Nicole's visit, our e-mail correspondence began and our friendship deepened as we learned more about each other and supported each other in prayer. Every day was filled with thoughts of Nicole. I daydreamed about being with her, helping with Nicholas, and providing for both of them. Something deep within me wanted to make everything better for her.

The more I thought about her, the more I desired for us to be together again, even if just for a brief visit. As I brainstormed, I remembered a friend's upcoming wedding in Atlanta. I asked Nicole to be my date, but in a nonthreatening "just friends" kind of way. I decided to guard my heart and be extremely careful not to be too open with my feelings—a fine balance between prudence and a fear of being rejected.

The weekend in Atlanta was amazing. We stayed with dear friends of mine and had plenty of time to talk and get better acquainted. In my mind, a shift was taking place. I no longer considered Nicole a *possible* mate. I had fallen in love with her. I did not see how a long-distance relationship could work, but I was willing to try to figure out something. I strategically sent subtle signals—foot rubs, hugs, and playful smiles—to display my growing affection. I even hid some gas money in her car without her knowing.

I didn't want the weekend to end, but soon enough, Nicole was in her car driving to Tennessee and I was boarding a plane to Minnesota. I spent the whole flight pouring my love into a letter.

When I got home, I decided to hold on to the letter a little while before sending it. The more I thought about the obstacles that stood in our way, the more I became convinced that the timing wasn't right to reveal my feelings to Nicole. Although my heart's desire remained constant, my hope dwindled. I could not see how, across the distance, we could build and maintain anything more than the relationship we already had as friends, so I tried to move on. I worked with plenty of other girls who were nice and attractive, but none measured up to Nicole.

When I heard about Nicole's move to North Dakota, my hope for a relationship with her was renewed. While a Minnesota/

Tennessee connection seemed impossible, a Minnesota/North Dakota connection was an altogether different story.

That fall, I saw her again and had the privilege of meeting Nicholas. Right away, he stole my heart with his blond hair and big, inquisitive blue eyes. We played and laughed until it was time for me to head home. He cried as I left; my heart was won.

Throughout the fall, I paid close attention to Nicole, trying to discern her feelings. As I did not sense any interest on her end, I resigned myself to the fact that we would just be good friends. Although saddened a little by this reality, the Lord brought me to a place of contentment in my walk with Him.

I saw Nicole and Nicholas over Christmas and, like before, did not perceive any romantic feelings toward me. I resigned my dreams of a relationship. In fact, when I returned to Minnesota after Christmas vacation, I planned to ask out a girl from my church who helped me teach English classes. I was at work late the night that I received Nicole's e-mail. Needless to say, I was completely shocked when I read the words that nearly mirrored the letter I had written a year earlier. I reread it several times to make sure I understood what she was saying. I got up from my desk and went for a walk to clear my head. I was terrified and exhilarated at the same time.

As I walked, I felt the weight of my decision. If it had been a normal situation (without any children involved), I would have jumped in without any hesitation. Nicole was the girl I had fallen in love with over a year ago. But the idea of being a husband and an instant father overwhelmed me. I didn't want to get attached to Nicole and Nicholas, only to end up leaving if things didn't work out. I realized that there would be no trial period with this relationship—it was all or nothing.

I responded to Nicole's e-mail and said I needed time to think, pray, and seek counsel before I could give her an answer. I knew what my heart wanted, but I needed confirmation in my mind and spirit. I asked several people for their advice. Some had been married for forty-five years, some for five years, and some were single. But they all knew me and were able to seek the Lord on my behalf.

As I received their counsel, I realized that not one of my friends gave me any reason not to pursue my heart. I did not talk to Nicole during this time because I wanted to hear clearly from God.

On New Year's Eve, I spent the night alone at church, praying and listening. I remembered the words I had heard from the Lord almost a year before: "I want you to marry this woman and take care of her." I pressed into God to see if He was still speaking those words to me.

I sent an e-mail to my pastor back home. Nicole was now attending his church, so I felt I could trust him with both of our hearts. His advice to me was this:

Dear Jon,

Thank you for your e-mail yesterday. Thank you for your confidence in sharing all the information you did. I will certainly keep it confidential (with the exception of Polly, who is a great prayer partner and my best friend—We'll be married forty-five years tomorrow).

It's really exciting to see how God has worked and continues to work in both your and Nicole's lives. Each Wednesday, Jim, Ed (Nicole's grandpa), and I meet together for prayer. Among the things we've been praying for is that the Lord would lead Nicole to a godly man who would be genuinely interested in her as a person and not just for her beauty. As Ed says, "She's a beautiful girl, probably too beautiful for her own good." In any event, I personally believe that you, Jon, have your head on straight and strive to honor the Lord.

I clearly sense that the Lord is leading in your lives. We will continue to pray for both of you that you might continue to sense God's leading, wisdom, understanding, and sensitivity to His will. I personally believe that both of you are on the right track.

Let me digress for a minute, Jon. When I was in high school and getting into college, I dated Polly a couple of times when we attended Camp Bentley. God placed within my heart a sense that she was the person for me, but I still dated a lot of other gals in high school and college. Somehow, I never had the feelings for any of them that I had for Polly. I hadn't seen Polly for quite a while and had been only in occasional correspondence with her.

When I was in the Navy, stationed in Hawaii, I heard that a friend of mine from seminary was doing summer work at Grace Baptist in Grand Forks. I knew he had an interest in Polly. So I prayed about the matter and then sent Polly a telegram asking her to marry me.

Needless to say, her response was affirmative. From then on, through almost daily correspondence, our relationship grew as we shared our lives with each other. Tomorrow, we celebrate our forty-fifth wedding anniversary. We thank God for the gift He has given to us in each other.

Jon, from what you've shared with me, I sense God is leading you two together. What an exciting time in your lives! Enjoy the ride, but keep looking to the Lord Jesus daily for His direction and affirmation. Don't rush into matters, but consider all the ramifications that being a spouse and an "instant" father involve.

This Sunday, I'm preaching a message titled "*A Magnificent Adventure.*" It's about some important things we can learn from the wise men who came from the east to visit the newborn King. One lesson is this: They were willing to follow wherever the star might lead.

I am by no means speaking as an authority on or as the epitome of life, Jon. But there are times when we have to take risks. As I say in my sermon, "If we are going to get anywhere in life, if we are going to achieve anything for our Lord Jesus and His kingdom, sooner or later we are going to have to go out on a limb."

There are a lot of risks in life. I'm sure you're aware of that. As you pursue a relationship with Nicole, there are risks involved. But with the sense of our Lord's leading in your lives, the risks are minimized.

I trust that what I've shared with you makes some sense. I'd like to leave you with a verse, well known to you, I'm sure.

Proverbs 3:5–6 (NIV). "Trust in the Lord with all your heart and lean not on your own understanding; in all your ways acknowledge him, and he will make your paths straight."

Be assured of our prayers for you and Nicole and Nicholas. We're excited for you and for the way in which our Lord will continue to direct your paths.

In Christ's love,

Pastor Bill

As I meditated on Pastor Bill's advice, I knew what my decision would be.

 Dreams Come True

It was a new year, and with each day I felt more and more peace about Jon and me. I hadn't heard anything from him other than his first e-mail, so I waited patiently. One afternoon at about two o'clock, a florist delivery van pulled up outside my office building. Since a badge was needed to get into the building, I met the deliveryman at the front door. I never imagined that he had come with something for me. So when he said, "I have a delivery for . . ." and the name that came out of his mouth was mine, I was a little dumbfounded.

"That's me!" I replied, and I signed his clipboard. He smiled as he handed me a long white box. I took the box to the nearest table and my coworkers quickly gathered around me to see what all the fuss was about. I opened the lid and saw a dozen beautiful red roses. I was twenty-three years old and had never received a dozen roses from anyone. I picked up the card and found only three words written on it: "Let's do it!"

I smiled and cried all at once. This was my biggest dream coming true!

As soon as my shift ended, I raced home to call my new *boyfriend*. When I called Jon, I heard relief in his voice. Because of my work schedule, the florist was unable to deliver the flowers for two days. Jon was worried that, since I hadn't responded, I might have changed my mind!

I must say, our first conversation as "sweethearts" was a little awkward, especially since it was on the phone. I planned a trip to visit him that weekend in Minnesota. Luckily, I had a three-day weekend ahead of me, and Grandma and Grandpa offered to care for Nicholas.

I arrived in Minneapolis at five o'clock in the evening, just as the sky was getting dark. I buzzed Jon from the lobby of his apartment building and waited for him to come down to get me. Through the glass door, I could see him jogging toward me. We were both giggling as he pushed open the door and picked me up into a timeless embrace. We grabbed my suitcase from the car and carried it upstairs. We had a few hours alone before his roommates returned. We talked and laughed, pinching ourselves throughout the evening to make sure it was all real.

Jon asked me about my hopes and dreams for the future. I opened up to him and shared with him the things I envisioned, how I never desired a career, but longed to stay home with Nicholas and focus on ministry (maybe even do some writing!). Jon listened intently, and with a warm smile, said, "I would love to make all those dreams come true."

That night, Jon let me sleep on his bed and he took the couch. We had an amazing whirlwind of a weekend—eating out, visiting, sharing our dreams, and, of course, cuddling. I could feel passion rising up within me every time I saw him.

My heart melted when he took me to his little Spanish-speaking church in downtown St. Paul. In college, Jon double majored in computer programming and Spanish. While studying abroad in Costa Rica, he fell in love with the Hispanic culture and made a point to reach out to immigrants when he returned to the US. When he graduated from college, he secured a job as a computer programmer and established a ministry of ESL

(English as a Second Language). Teaching English was his evangelistic tool and he absolutely loved it. When I got to see him in action that weekend, I rejoiced in his heart for the people. His heart was for missions and Hispanic people and mine was for single moms. Our common denominator was a desire to burn for Jesus.

During that weekend, we shared our hearts with each other. The most amazing thing Jon told me was this: Before the two of us had seriously considered a romantic relationship, he had felt a growing desire to adopt a child. Now, how many single, twenty-four-year-old men do you know are eager to adopt and raise a child on their own? I saw how God had put the desire in Jon's heart to prepare him for Nicholas! It was so obvious. The last key was in place. Jon's desire was so extraordinary that I knew God had orchestrated our relationship. I had prayed so many times that God would place Nicholas on the heart of his future father, and He had faithfully answered my prayers!

After I returned home, Jon and I kept in very close touch (to the extent of nine to ten e-mails a day!). He decided to come see me for my birthday on January 14. He was anxious to see Nicholas and reconnect with him and the rest of my family.

When he arrived in North Dakota, Nicholas and Jon played for hours in the snow. As I watched them interact, I was amazed at how much they loved each other and how naturally they got along.

Nicholas fell asleep in Ruby's arms as she read him his favorite book. Jon and I went into the family room to cuddle up by the wood-burning stove. Even on such a bitterly cold night, I could have not felt more heat!

After years of waiting, my Boaz had come at last. I was living my dream. At times it almost seemed too fantastic to be real. As we savored the night in each other's arms, hours passed. Jon turned to me with a sudden burst of energy and asked, "What would you say if I told you I had a ring for you in my pocket?"

With a huge smile on my face, I replied, "I'd say there is no way you have a ring in your pocket!" Jon had never in his life rushed into major decisions; he was an extremely cautious, calculated, responsible young man. He did love adventure, but a proposal was just unthinkable. We had only officially been together for two weeks! Yet his question definitely spurred my curiosity.

After nearly thirty minutes of teasing and joking back and forth, Jon got up, walked over to his coat, and grabbed something out of one of the pockets. He came back to where I was sitting. I sat up, noticing the seriousness in his face. The house was silent as everyone slept. The fire crackled behind him. As he got down on one knee, I could feel waves of intense emotion flow through me. Just as my life changed forever when Nicholas entered the world, so it was about to change again. Jon looked at me with adoration as he pulled out a silver band. He said, "This is not a ring I bought for you; it's my ring that I bought in Costa Rica. It is all I had time to arrange for until I could buy you a diamond engagement ring." My eyes widened and my heart nearly exploded as he took my hand. Tears rolled down my face as he asked, "Nicole, will you be my wife?"

A thousand yeses echoed through my mind before one actually came out of my mouth. With more love than I had ever felt and through many tears of joy, I fell into his arms and cried out, "Yes!"

Conclusion

By keeping testimonies correct and by sharing them diligently, we are filled with *courage* to believe in a God who intervenes and makes *impossible situations possible*. Here is my personal and heartfelt prayer for you, my dear reader.

> Jesus, I thank You from the bottom of my heart for finding me and saving me and making all my dreams come true. Your love for me truly is remarkable. I also thank You for placing my book in this amazing woman's hands. Your love for her is incredible. I ask that You would do for her what You did for me. I thank You for giving her the hope she needs and for granting the desires of her heart. You truly are the Lover of our souls. Let the miracle that is my life now become hers. Amen.

Acknowledgments

I have so many people to thank, I struggle with where to begin. Through many tears of joy, I will first mention my personal Savior, Jesus Christ. To You I owe my life, to You I owe my service. Without You, there would be no happy ending. Without You, there would be no story worthy of sharing. You are the light of my life, and I will serve You all of my days.

To my amazing husband: Your encouragement has lifted me to heights I did not know I could reach. You are my hero. Your love for me has molded me into the woman I've always aspired to be. From the day of our wedding, not a week has passed that I did not stop and thank God for the gift He gave me in you. Your passion for me causes me to want to be a better person. Your love for our children melts my heart. You believed in me when no one else cared. You were willing to sacrifice yourself to see me walk into my destiny. Your servant heart has blessed me through and through. Your love for the Lord inspires me, and I will never take you for granted.

To Nicholas: I often thank God for your unexpected arrival in my life. Who knows where I would be if there hadn't been you!

To Caleb and Jeremiah: God has blessed me abundantly through you, my strapping young boys. My prayer is that I will be able to help both of you find your destinies in Christ.

To Mom and Dad: You gave me life and I love you very much. Thank you for all the sacrifices you made while raising me. I treasure the restored relationship we now have and look forward to many years of happiness.

To Kim, Susan, Ruby, Gerald, Cemanthia, Rich, Rob, Sunny, Sheri, Danny, grandmas and grandpas, aunts and uncles, cousins and classmates, pastors and counselors: You all contributed to who I am today. I thank you sincerely for believing in me and helping me accomplish my goal of writing this book.

To order additional copies of

Have your credit card ready and call

Toll free: (877) 421-READ (7323)

or order online at:
www.survivingsinglemotherhood.com
or
www.winepressbooks.com